AROUND THE WORLD IN SIXTY YEARS

SIGNPOSTS IN TAXCO, MEXICO
ELIJAH-LOVKOFF/ISTOCKPHOTO

LIBRARY OF CONGRESS CATALOGING-IN-PUBLICATION DATA PENDING
WOLFE, JOHN S., AROUND THE WORLD IN SIXTY YEARS:
THE EXPERIENCES AND WISDOM OF A GENERATION OF
GENTLEMEN FROM ARGENTINA TO ZIMBABWE
ISBN 979-8-9916198-0-6
COVER DESIGN AND LAYOUT BY CAMERON HOOD
MAPS AND GRAPHICS BY SANJAY DHUNGANA
PRINTED IN THE UNITED STATES

AROUND THE WORLD IN SIXTY YEARS

THE EXPERIENCES AND WISDOM OF A GENERATION
OF GENTLEMEN FROM ARGENTINA TO ZIMBABWE

JOHN S. WOLFE

CONTENTS

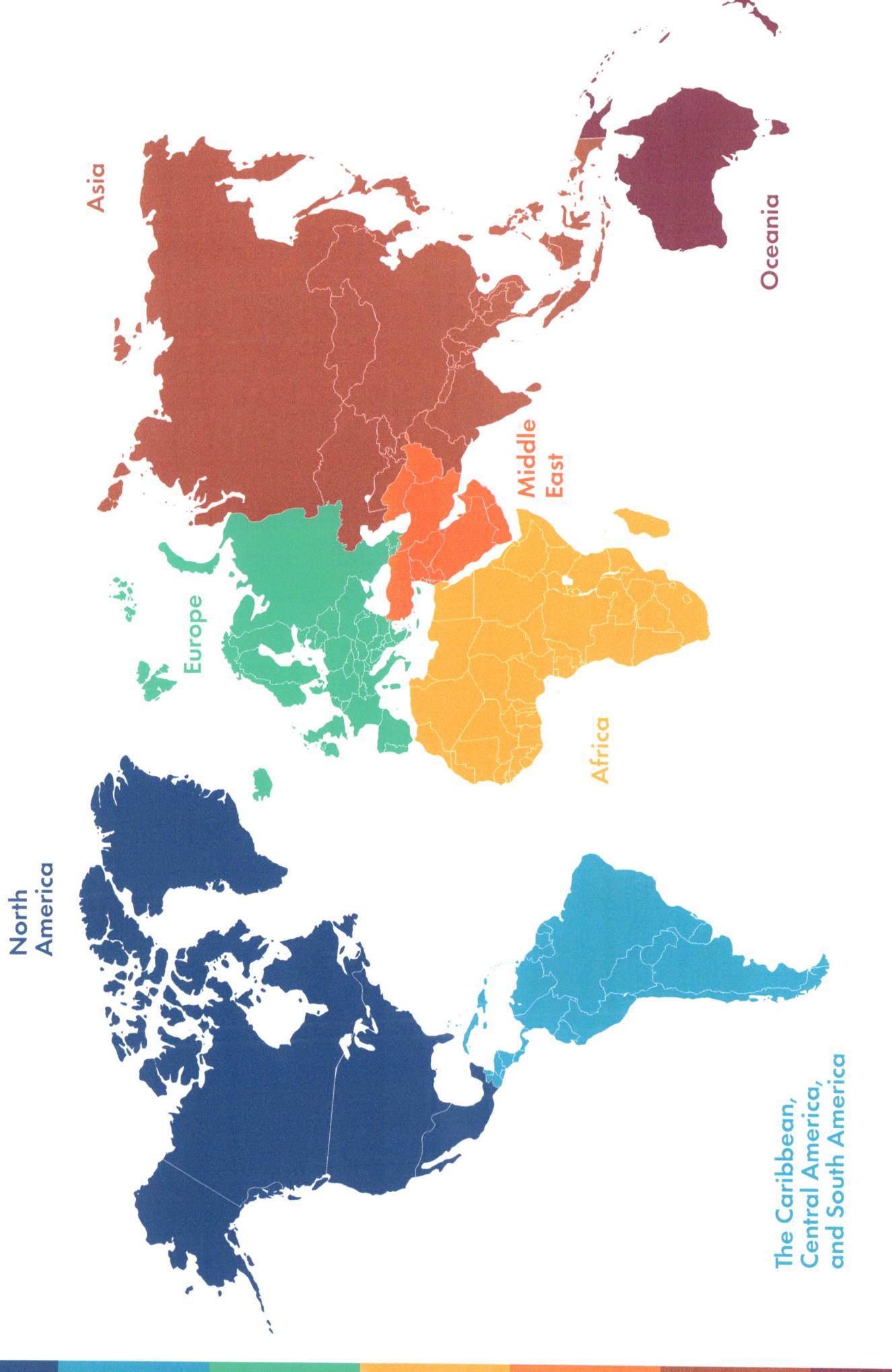

ACKNOWLEDGMENTS

THIS PROJECT DOESN'T GET COMPLETED WITHOUT
THE HELP OF A LOT OF PEOPLE.

■ **AM GRATEFUL** to the gentlemen around the world who indulged an American far away to participate in *Around the World in Sixty Years*.

Gratitude to my family and friends, especially my wife Michelle, who encouraged this endeavor and continues to inspire me. Thank you to Christina, Lien, Chelsea, Jacob, Giulia, Celine, Picha, Cagla, Amira and Kamilla; Scott and Lorrie; Michael; B.J., Charlene, Oscar, Nomi, Sam, Luca, Bell, Titus, Wendy, Terry, Alvin and Vanessa. From the *Queen Victoria* cruise, special thanks to Brian Marova and Chillie Stent-Wardell.

Special recognition goes to the men and women far, far away who took a chance responding to a strange email and then proceeded to help me locate participants in my demographic. These helpful individuals were: Melanie Middleton in New Zealand, Frances in Fiji, Berna Kalenci Lee in South Korea, Andres Izquierdo Bacarreza in Chile, Beny Wilson Altamiranda in Panama, Karolina Klesta in

Poland, Simon Pozek in Slovenia, Klara Konicarova in the Czech Republic, Henry Nguyen in Vietnam, and Julie Gilders in Spain.

Last, but not least, this wouldn't have been possible without the assistance and support of tour companies and tour guides around the world. They are a valuable group — outgoing, friendly, helpful, knowledgeable, and worldly. If they couldn't participate, they knew someone who knew someone who might. If you have any plans to visit these countries, please consider contacting these individuals to arrange a tour:

- Samantha "Sam" Clooney of the Association of Tour Guides in Ireland
- Alexandra Godowski of Who Is Amsterdam
- Samantha Aeschbach of the Zurich Insider
- Anna Geisler of Anna Loves Vienna
- Callum Chiverton of The Real France
- Merritt Howertown of Roar Africa in Kenya
- Muluken Girma of Meet Mule in Ethiopia

- Estimic Visiri and Miriam Kyasiimire of Kagera Safaris in DR Congo
- Abdeslam Abira of IMoroc-co Tours in Morocco
- Thabelo Thathani of Itani Tours in South Africa
- Santosh Prashad Rimal in Nepal
- Takuzo Muneshige of Japan
- Kaori Noda of Happy Happy Tokyo
- Paula Morgan of Sydney Expert
- Valur Heidar Saevarsson of Your Friend in Reykjavik
- Alexander Pina of Cape Verde
- Peter Chrenka of Authentic Slovakia
- Kaisa Heiskari of the Apukka Resort in Finland

I would also like to thank my graphic artist, Sanjay Dhungana in Nepal, and my publishing artist, Cameron Hood of Tucson, for making the vision into a reality.

ABOUT THIS BOOK

"WERE YOU, BY CHANCE, BORN IN 1964?" I TENTATIVELY ASKED. "CAN I INQUIRE WHY YOU WANT TO KNOW?" THE GENTLEMAN RESPONDED. AND THAT IS HOW THE AROUND THE WORLD IN SIXTY YEARS BOOK PROJECT BEGAN.

I T WAS JAN. 11, 2023 and my wife, Michelle, and I had entered the slightly chilly waiting area at the Southampton cruise terminal. We were about to embark on the *Queen Victoria,* which was being prepped to begin a special centennial world voyage for the Cunard cruise line.

It would be a once-in-a-lifetime experience for us — a 100-day voyage that would begin and end along the coast of southern England. That evening we would begin to head west — to the United States, to the breezy Caribbean, through the Panama Canal, and across the Pacific to summertime in Australia. Then the ship would sail north to humid Singapore and ports in between, then cross the Indian Ocean to the gleaming skylines of the United Arab Emirates, and through the Suez Canal into the Mediterranean Sea. The voyage would conclude with stops in Naples, Italy and Lisbon, Portugal before arriving back in England on April 23.

After running a gift shop in Chandler, Arizona for 11 years, this was a "bucket list" gift to ourselves. We would be together every day in a small stateroom for the next three months — but, then again, we had been married for 36 years so that wouldn't be a problem.

Now retired and approaching my 60th birthday in 2024, I mulled how to use my journalism background to make the voyage more memorable.

I could do some travel writing in different ports or document the day-to-day activities on a cruise ship. I then thought, wouldn't it be interesting if I could meet men my age around the world and get their perspectives on life at 60. That would be fun, a bit of a challenge, but it wouldn't consume all of my time at sea.

With Michelle's help I developed a questionnaire. The original one was 28 questions. That was way too many for any gentleman I might be able to persuade to take part. We whittled it down to 12 questions. Then we departed Arizona.

At the Southampton cruise terminal, we were welcomed by Lucien De-Laloi, a friendly and nattily dressed agent. He provided some boarding information and we sat down to wait.

Then I looked at him and thought, *He looks about my age.*

I followed him to another aisle and posed the question I would repeat dozens of times in the coming months.

"Yes, I was born in 1964," Lucien responded. I explained my project and he said it sounded interesting. I took his photo in the terminal and he gave me his email address. I sent him the questions and within a couple of weeks he had responded with lengthy, thoughtful answers. *This might work,* I thought.

Tour guides became great resources and sometimes subjects. Gusti Gunawan, our guide in Bali, Indonesia, was so enthusiastic that he returned his questionnaire three hours after I emailed it to him.

The more I saw of the world, the more convinced I was that this project had merit beyond just personality profiles. I was seeing similarities among gentlemen in different countries, on different continents, and of different socioeconomic backgrounds.

After the voyage, I tapped all of my high school friends, college friends, professional colleagues, Michelle's friends, my children's contacts, and our foreign-exchange daughters to identify candidates in countries we didn't visit. The participation total rose to about 25. But the project needed more breadth.

At the beginning of 2024 I started to look for participants through Facebook groups, LinkedIn connections and emails to tour companies, bloggers, birding associations and genealogy organizations. Not everyone responded but the approach did lead me to gentlemen in places like New Zealand, Poland, the Philippines and even Nepal. Success!

As the replies came in, with photos of men my age around the world, it became clear that serendipity had produced an array of gentlemen of all professions, ethnicities, faiths and families. It became clear that, despite the attention conflicts receive, we all have much in common when it comes to priorities in life. That's the message of this book.

One last point . . . I had a number of women in my outreach effort ask why they couldn't be involved. I replied, first, it wouldn't be safe for my health to approach women in different countries and ask their age. And, second, by keeping with the male gender, it was a common denominator for bringing all of the profiles together.

Finally, I told them, if this goes well, the next book will be from the female point of view — and I will be contacting you!

Thanks for your interest in this book. If you would like to become involved, please contact me.

— JOHN

www.aroundtheworldbooks.org
facebook.com/aroundtheworldbook
aroundtheworldbook1964@gmail.com

IN REVIEWING THE PBS DOCUMENTARY *1964*, THE NON-PROFIT WEBSITE NEXT AVENUE GAVE THE YEAR A SUBTITLE: "THE YEAR AMERICA LOST IT."

I WAS THE YEAR American culture fractured and eventually split along ideological lines — old *vs.* young, hip *vs.* square, poor *vs.* rich, liberal *vs.* conservative — establishing the poles of societal debate that are still raging today," Tad Simons wrote in 2014.

America was in the acceptance phase that President John F. Kennedy had been assassinated in Dallas and replaced by a crass Texan hand-shaker in Lyndon B. Johnson.

1964 was a presidential election year in the United States and President Johnson pursued legislative successes and achieved them: the Civil Rights Act of 1964, to end discrimination on basis of race, color, religion or national origin, and the Economic Opportunity Act of 1964, part of Johnson's "Great Society" agenda to end poverty.

His year also featured the August aggression by the North Vietnamese in the Gulf of Tonkin, which led President Johnson to increase American firepower in Vietnam to respond to the commu-

nist threat. Active U.S. combat troops would arrive there in 1965.

The summer of 1964 is remembered for destructive race riots in urban areas like Harlem in New York City; Rochester, New York; Dixmoor, Illinois; and Philadelphia. Acts of discrimination, police aggressiveness, and chronic unemployment fueled the uprisings, which would be replicated in other cities in the following four summers.

1964 also saw the honoring of Dr. Martin Luther King Jr. with the Nobel Peace Prize.

1964 | *Around the World in Sixty Years*

64

His famous "I have a dream" speech had culminated in the "March on Washington for Jobs and Freedom" in August 1963.

THE YEAR IN THE UNITED STATES IS ALSO REMEMBERED FOR THESE HIGHLIGHTS:

- 1964 marked the arrival in the United States of The Beatles, who performed on *The Ed Sullivan Show* on three consecutive Sundays in February.

- The U.S. surgeon general declared for the first time that smoking is hazardous to your health.

- The Organization of Afro-American Unity.

- Malcolm X left the Nation of Islam and formed a black nationalism organization, the

- 22-year-old Cassius Clay upset Sonny Liston on Feb. 25, 1964 to become the world heavyweight champion boxer. A week later he would announce himself as Muhammad Ali.

- The *Jeopardy* game show debuted on NBC. The castaways on *Gilligan's Island* were exiled on CBS.

- Black-and-white television was about to become "Technicolor."

- The Rolling Stones released their debut album.

- The most powerful earthquake in U.S. history — with a magnitude 9.2 on the Richter scale — devastated Anchorage, Alaska.

- The Berkeley Free Speech Movement began on the California campus with civil disobedience to allow free speech and political activities.

- Sidney Poitier became the first African-American to win an Academy Award. He received the Best Actor honor for his role in *Lilies of the Field*.

- The Verrazzano-Narrows bridge connecting the New York City boroughs of Brooklyn and Staten Island opened.

- Ford introduced the Mustang sports car.

- *Sports Illustrated* published its first "swimsuit issue."

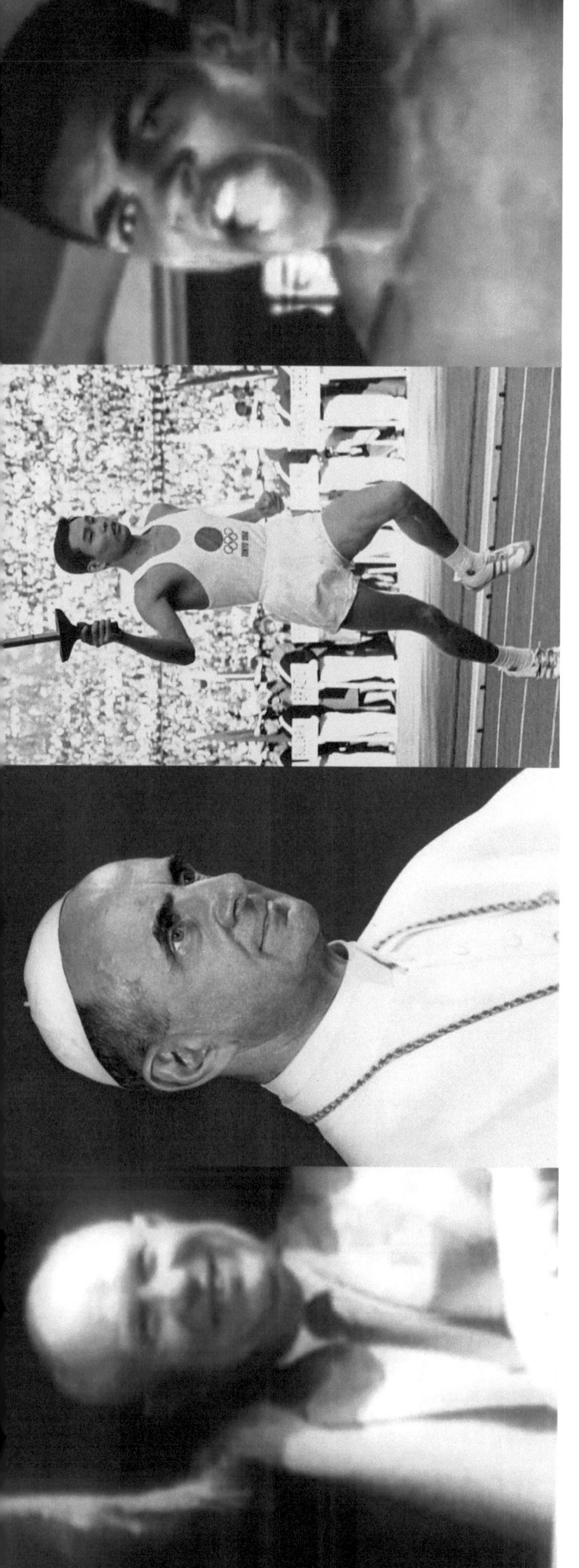

NOTEWORTHY EVENTS IN 1964 AROUND THE WORLD:

- The military in Brazil led a coup against President Joao Goulart. The resulting dictatorship would end in 1985.

- India's first prime minister, Jawaharlal Nehru, died of a heart attack, ending his 16-year tenure in the newly independent republic.

- Japan introduced the world's first high-speed rail line between Tokyo and Osaka.

- The Soviet Union's Politburo deposed Nikita Khrushchev and replaced him with Leonid Brezhnev.

- Greeks and Turks fought over Cyprus, which had gained independence from the United Kingdom in 1960.

- The International Olympic Committee banned South Africa from participating in the Tokyo Games because of its segregated team. The Summer Games were the first Olympics held in Asia.

- France and the People's Republic of China established diplomatic relations. Taiwan (the Republic of China) cut ties with France.

- The conflict between Indonesia and newly formed Malaysia — from British colonies — intensified, with Commonwealth forces defending the new country

- The "traveling pontiff," Pope Paul VI, visited Jerusalem, India, and Colombia and oversaw the Ecumenical Council, which addressed church reforms. The stay in Jerusalem included the first meeting between the Pope and the leader of the Orthodox Church in 500 years.

- Canada adopted a new flag featuring a maple leaf.

- Nelson Mandela, who had been imprisoned in South Africa in 1962, gave his "I am prepared to die" speech on April 20, 1964 at the Rivonia trial.

- The island of Malta in the Mediterranean Sea gained independence from the United Kingdom.

- The country of Rhodesia disintegrated. (It is now Zimbabwe and Zambia.) There was unrest in Uganda, Kenya, Zanzibar and Tanganyika. Congo — formerly Belgium's — saw bloodshed from revolution.

B

UT IF YOU WERE BORN IN 1964, YOU EXPERIENCED NONE OF THIS.

You learned about the Apollo program, Woodstock, hippies, civil rights, the Cold War between the United States and Soviet Union, the Cuban missile crisis, political assassinations, Vietnam, Nixon, antiwar protests, the Six-Day War between Israel and Egypt in 1967, China's "Cultural Revolution," the "pill," and the National Organization for Women from television, movies, books, newspapers, and magazines.

In the United States, the 1970s provided some memories of adolescence, probably related to television shows like *M*A*S*H* or *Happy Days* or movies like *Star Wars* or *Jaws.* You can remember adults talking about gas lines, Watergate, Jimmy Carter and inflation but that wasn't of interest to most teens. Rock music was not the Beatles or Led Zeppelin or The Who; it was more like Queen, Aerosmith, Styx and the Eagles.

The 1980s was adulthood — Reaganomics, power suits, Michael Jackson, Wall Street mergers, Gorbachev, Chernobyl, cable television, the space shuttle disaster, Madonna and AIDS. Maybe you started a family. Maybe you waited.

Around the World in Sixty Years is an attempt to fill in the blanks for the subsequent decades with gentlemen across the continents.

From Bali to Zimbabwe, Poland to Panama, these are the stories of gentlemen born around 1964.

NORTH AMERICA

UNLIKE THOSE IN OTHER PARTS OF THE WORLD, NORTH AMERICA'S LAST 60 YEARS CAN BE DESCRIBED IN ONE WORD: STABLE.

SURE, Canada has faced the issue of the secession of the province of Québec. Mexico has seen political turmoil but only in the framework of its constitutional republic. The United States has been so uncontentious that the two opposing political parties have been derided as the "uni-party" of common interests and, more significantly, explosive spending by the government.

So what would characterize this continent since the 1960s?

Changing demographics of the population. Immigration — legal and illegal. Transitions from manufacturing economies to service and high-tech economies in the United States and Canada. Social upheavals over foreign wars, civil rights, women's rights, and income inequality, culminating in the divisions created by the Covid-19 pandemic and work and school lockdowns of 2020.

Going back to the 1960s, the United States has been at the forefront of aerospace advances, computer technology, music and film industries, the introduction of the cellphone, global banking and markets, and, of course, the introduction of the internet. Canada's and Mexico's proximities to this have been advantageous.

It also helps that the three nations have what many others don't — an abundance of land. Canada is the second largest country on Earth, behind Russia but ahead of China. The United States is the fourth largest. Mexico is the 14th largest.

That territory provides resources and opportunities for both companies and individuals.

United States

Ron Cooper

Place of Birth:
Rochester, New York, United States

Current Residence:
Greece, New York, United States

What is the best thing about where you live?

The best thing about Rochester is the summer weather and the variety of festivals and activities available.

How has life changed in your country since you were a child?

The biggest change has been the increase in awareness and acceptance of diverse populations. As a child, I was aware of limitations placed on me because of the color of my skin. I was also aware of the blatant prejudice against African Americans.

What has been the most important event in your country in your lifetime?

The Covid-19 pandemic.

How has your view of work changed over time?

Starting my first job I felt accomplished. I was proud knowing I had achieved the first of my goals and had been chosen out of a significant number of applicants. I looked forward to learning new things and the new challenges that would come up each day. I found a sense of fulfillment in my work. Recently my department was outsourced and the increase in administrative demands has created a monotony, making me feel discontented and looking forward to retirement and the opportunity to do something new.

Tell me about your family:

I have been happily married for almost 23 years. My wife and I have two daughters. One is in college pursuing a degree in adolescent psychology. Our younger daughter is a senior in high school. My children from my first marriage live in North Carolina and Florida. My son is currently the head athletic trainer for the North Carolina State University men's basketball team and my daughter is a manager for a pharmaceutical company. I am so proud of all they have accomplished and the quality people they have become.

What is the most important lesson your family taught you?

My wife, Jody, has taught me to be confident in who I am but to always keep growing. She encourages me and has taught me to look for the positives, even in the midst of challenges.

What is your biggest fear?

Dying and not being there for my family.

What is your greatest pride?

I am most proud of being the first in my family to attend and graduate from college.

What was the favorite time of your life?

High school. It was a fun time with no responsibilities and no worries. I loved playing basketball and football and hanging out with friends. It was such a carefree time compared to the stresses of adulthood.

What is the best decision you made?

The best decision in my life was getting screened for prostate cancer at only 45 years old. My doctor didn't order the test, but if I had not had it checked, I most likely would not be here today.

Do you have a hidden talent?

If the band Earth, Wind & Fire needed me, I could jump right in!

What advice do you have for the next generation?

My advice would be to always work hard; nothing is given to you. Always treat people the way you want to be treated and always look for ways to grow to become the best version of yourself.

United States
Edward Bailey Hodgman

Place of Birth:
Rochester, New York, United States

Current Residence:
Rockville, Maryland, United States

What is the best thing about where you live?

I am very fortunate to live in a peaceful and relatively safe community. Rockville is a fairly typical small American city. Though it is right outside of Washington, D.C., it isn't influenced much by the fights over national politics happening just a few miles away.

And the state of Maryland is an interesting place. A small state by American standards, it has both ocean and mountains, large cities and small towns, and a proud heritage created by different religions and cultures.

How has life changed in your country since you were a child?

What has changed the most in America since I was a child is what has changed the most for everyone in the world: the sweeping introduction of immediate information flows into people's lives via modern digital technologies.

If you were to take away the internet and cellphones, most things would probably be much the same as when I was a boy in Upstate New York.

But with the introduction — the intrusion — the inescapable influence — of digital technologies, the rhythms of life have changed irreversibly.

Our daily lives have been changed in ways that would make some of our attitudes and behaviors hard for people who lived before the internet to understand.

What has been the most important event in your country in your lifetime?

There have been many important historical events, from Watergate to America's loss in Vietnam to the end of the Cold War. But the most important, all-encompassing event in my country in my lifetime has been the introduction of the smartphone into people's daily lives.

How has your view of work changed over time?

When I was just starting out, I was ambitious for the sake of ambition. I thought I needed to be important, influential, and well-known. But relatively early in my career, I realized that if I were to seek a position of power, it would open the door to the vanity and greed that are, unfortunately, part of my character.

So instead of going into politics, I focused more on working in business and on helping build companies. I have not become an amazing success in anything I have done, but by working intensively with people (both clients and my colleagues) I have achieved a real sense of fulfillment, and work that changes every day. I still wonder if I should have gone into politics or worked in government. But I'm content with what I have and I enjoy what I do.

Tell me about your family:

I am now married for the second time. My first marriage lasted more than 25 years, and I am now part of two families — my old one and my new one.

I feel like my children are in the middle of a Venn diagram — the overlapping space between my new and old families — with all the challenges that brings.

My family has changed due to the death of my father, who was very important to me. I am blessed that my mother is still alive. My three sisters are wonderful people I continue to learn from and enjoy knowing.

Without a doubt, my new wife is the love of my life and I feel very fortunate to have met her. I also still care for my first wife and want her to be happy. Getting divorced and marrying again is something I never imagined for myself, but it's a wonderful change and has made my life better.

What is the most important lesson that your family taught you?

Patience. I have no doubt that the way I have lived my life over the years has helped my family learn patience, too!

What's your biggest fear?

That the love of violence that is part of the human condition will erupt into wars that will lead to the end of life as we know it.

What is your greatest pride?

That I have helped my children mature into adulthood as kind and thoughtful people.

What was the favorite time of your life?

I love my life right now, but by far the most thrilling and varied part of my life was living and working in the old Soviet Union in the era of perestroika and glasnost.

What is the best decision you made?

Learning Russian.

Do you have a hidden talent?

Using humor to reduce tension in interpersonal relations. Though the way I just said that doesn't sound funny at all.

What advice do you have for the next generation?

Unplug. That doesn't mean unplug forever, or at all times. It means unplug when you can and explore the world without the help of modern technologies.

If you unplug and think and feel, with all the pain that real thinking and feeling brings, it will make you more able to achieve Shakespeare's challenge to the ages in "Hamlet," whose stunning force is best understood by reading it in full: "This above all: to thine own self be true, and it must follow, as the night the day, thou canst not then be false to any man."

NEAR ROCKVILLE, MARYLAND, UNITED STATES

ANDRES HERRERA/UNSPLASH

United States

Jay Phillips

Place of Birth:
Rochester, New York, United States

Current Residence:
Cookeville, Tennessee, United States

What is the best thing about where you live?

I'm with my oldest son and lovely wife and five grandkids!

How has life changed in your country since you were a child?

It was once generally safe and people, for the most part, were trustworthy and respectful — even if we disagreed or held vastly different opinions.

What has been the most important event in your country in your lifetime?

For sure and with no close comparison, it was the pandemic and its effect on our employment, cultural, political and social changes worldwide.

How has your view of work changed over time?

I wish I had planned better, prepared more, and been more consistent and more focused with more schooling.

Tell me about your family:

The beautiful and best part of my life. Five boys and two girls, now all adults and doing just fine. Six of the seven are married. Our 11th grandchild is due in June of 2024.

What is the most important lesson that your family taught you?

Life is precious and it goes so fast — so enjoy it! Make the best of it! It's only one shot!

What's your biggest fear?

I really do not live with much fear. I do, however, struggle with some anxiety that if I were to die well before my bride, that I will not have saved enough to provide for her needs.

What is your greatest pride?

My children and grandchildren, for sure.

What was the favorite time of your life?

The present. There have been some really good times and seasons, but it is incredible to be healthy and to be able to visit with my own children as adults. To see the grandkids as much as we do is awesome!

What is the best decision you made?

To become a Christian.

Do you have a hidden talent?

Remodeling and construction. Cooking.

What advice do you have for the next generation?

Should anyone of any future generation — or anyone at all — want my general advice on life, I would say the Scriptures have *all* that you may need. Go there! Not to me. Get to know the God who asserts to have made you, knows you, and loves you. So much so, that He gave His only son for you. My advice is to start with the Gospel of John, rather than starting with Genesis. May God be as gracious, merciful, forgiving and loving to you as He has to me.

United States

Stephen Kaufman

Place of Birth:
Wilmington, Delaware, United States

Current Residence:
Jacksonville, Florida, United States

What is the best thing about where you live?
A tie among three things:

- The weather, the people, the politics and its potential for growth.

- My daughter, whom I call "my pride and joy," and that I've helped her keep fighting through a serious illness.

- My work life: a 30-plus-year business and 27-year career as Navy Reserve officer.

- Finding love with Lisa — a deep, committed love I've heard described but never experienced till now.

What was the favorite time of your life?
Lots of good times but I'm hoping my "favorite" is still to come!

What is the best decision you made?
A tie between buying my first house at age 25 and running for the U.S. Congress. (Even though I lost the race, I won a new life with Lisa, who was my campaign manager.)

Do you have a hidden talent?
Yes . . . but nothing I can share publicly!

What advice do you have for the next generation?
Time truly flies — it is your greatest asset, and never forget your time here is limited. So work hard, take chances, find your dream and pursue it, and strive always to be a person who never says, "I woulda, coulda, shoulda." You get one life here — use it wisely!

What is your greatest pride?

How has life changed in your country since you were a child?
People just seem meaner, ruder, less civilized. I believe social media is the primary culprit.

What has been the most important event in your country in your lifetime?
9/11.

How has your view of work changed over time?
It really hasn't; some people do get lucky and succeed without much effort, but for most of us, it's hard work that enables us to achieve our goals. I feel so blessed to be working in my chosen field — even on the hardest days. I feel dang lucky.

Tell me about your family:
Divorced, one 20-something daughter, and I'm planning to be married later this year or early 2025 to my life partner, Lisa.

What is the most important lesson that your family taught you?
Unconditional love. I really didn't understand it until our daughter was born…truly life-changing.

What's your biggest fear?
I'll die before making a significant difference in this world.

United States

Tasúnka Akan Wicácte

("Kills on Horseback" in Lakota, "Jim Warne" in English)

Place of Birth:
Turtle Island (now known as the United States). Born in Phoenix, Arizona, United States.

Current Residence:
San Diego, California, United States

What is the best thing about where you live?

The ocean and year-round weather of San Diego.

I knew that I wanted to live here when I was on the Arizona State University football team and played in the 1985 Holiday Bowl in San Diego.

I moved here in 1989, earned my master's degree at San Diego State University in 1993, and ended up working at SDSU for 22 years. I live by Mission Bay and have a view of Ocean Beach.

How has life changed in your country since you were a child?

America continues to evolve and the pendulum swings with various degrees. Currently the pendulum has had momentum with extremes.

What has been the most important event in your country in your lifetime?

Due to segregation in Rapid City, SD, my parents moved to Arizona before I was born in 1964. That was the year the Civil Rights Act was enacted; the Indian Civil Rights Act passed in 1968. These events provided legal and federal precedence for Tribal Sovereignty.

The Indian Self-Determination and Education Assistance Act of 1975 ensured sovereign tribal government-to-government relationships required by federal law.

How has your view of work changed over time?

As a grandfather, and being trained in the Lakota Way, it is my responsibility to teach and share traditional ways of knowing to help influence our future generations.

My early work was the pursuit of childhood and youthful dreams of professional football and Hollywood film acting. I was fortunate to experience professional football, acting, and being a stuntman in several films.

As my life experience changed as a young adult — particularly when my son, Ryan, was born in 1993 — I began my career as an educator and advocate for indigenous disability and public health disparities in the university systems and Tribal Nations. This was life-changing, to work with the multitude of Tribal Nations and indigenous communities throughout the United States. I experienced the growth of these programs firsthand in creating employment outcomes for tribal members with disabilities.

A few years ago, I returned to the film industry as a producer, writer, and director so I could control the narrative and portrayal of our people.

Tell me about your family:

My brother, Don, and I were very fortunate to have the parents that we did.

My mom, Beverly Stabber Warne, recently made her journey to the spirit world and left many footprints for future generations in nursing and public health. She was an advocate, educator, healthcare provider, elder knowledge-keeper, and *uncí* (grandma) to many in the community.

My father, Jim Warne Sr., was an inspiration in many ways. He was a good man and provided an example of a strong person with respect for his wife and family. When faced with significant challenges, he continued to move forward.

When I was in high school, he was diagnosed with Multiple Sclerosis and estimated to have 10 years to live. He continued to live with MS for 37 years, continuing to work and not make it what defined him. I saw the man and not the wheelchair. I always say, "The strongest man I know just happened to use a wheelchair."

I was a single father with my boy, Ryan, and did well with family support. Fatherhood is a great responsibility, and I love the relationship I have with my boy, my son.

Then things completely changed when a woman named Jill literally walked into the room at a grant-writing conference where I was one of the instructors. She was representing her tribe, the Hoopa. I said *woah* to myself and little did I know that it would be a lifelong *woah*! We have been together for almost 30 years and enjoy our role as grandparents.

She is a tribal leader, an advocate, and a strong woman who represents her family and people in a good way. I am fortunate to have her in my life. Now, I'm a grandfather. Becoming "GG" has been wonderful and has helped influence another generation within my family.

What is the most important lesson that your family taught you?

To represent our ancestors in a good way. This life is not about me or you as an individual but is about us as a collective and what we can do to make it better for those who follow.

The ancestors watch our actions and want us to follow a good path... just as they did for us.

What's your biggest fear?

The future for our young ones, especially in our indigenous communities where they face significant challenges. The life expectancy, suicide, disability, and school dropout rates — and so many other environmental restrictions placed on our youth — are scary. They need to know their lives matter to those who will follow them.

What is your greatest pride?

Our young ones! Especially my son and my grandchildren. With all the challenges and odds against so many of our youth in "Indian Country," I continue to see many succeed.

Black Elk, an Oglala Lakota spiritual man, said it would take seven generations to heal our circle — our sacred hoop — and that is the children of today. Our young ones that know who they are speak our language and have been raised with an indigenous lens.

Many are graduating from college, performing in athletics, acting, studying academics, and working in industries at a high level. They are young leaders that know the importance of our Tribal Sovereignty.

What was the favorite time of your life?

Wow, as I look back on the journey of my life through each phase, I truly have been fortunate to have family support to live my dreams and to represent the *oyate*...the people.

What is the best decision you made?

Education, hands down! Thank you, mom and dad! Academia has provided me a platform to educate and share indigenous knowledge and ways of knowing with our young ones and our non-Indian educators and students as well.

Do you have a hidden talent?

I am an Emmy-nominated filmmaker and continue to make films today. I specialize in documentary films telling our stories from an indigenous perspective.

As a retired professional football player, I have conducted several football and life skills camps for thousands of indigenous youths at various Tribal Nations throughout the country.

What advice do you have for the next generation?

We are taught we represent seven generations behind and seven generations ahead. How will you represent your family and people seven generations behind and seven generations ahead?

This is a responsibility we all share as human beings, whether you are Lakota or non-Indian; as "two-legged" we must represent as best we can. Footprints, wheel prints, walker prints, prosthetic prints — whatever prints you leave should serve our future generations in a good way. Collectively, if we all leave a few "prints," we can make positive impact for our future generations.

As a grandfather I am fortunate to see four generations through my parents, myself, my son, and my grandkids. If I'm lucky, I will see a fifth before I make my ultimate journey.

The only guarantee we all share is that we all will make that ultimate journey. With that guarantee...what footprint will you leave?

Pilamayaye. (Thank you.)

MISSION BEACH, SAN DIEGO, CALIFORNIA, UNITED STATES

NICHOLAS/ADOBE STOCK

United States

David Gordon McIntyre

Place of Birth:
Los Angeles, California, United States

Current Residence:
San Jose, California, United States

What is the best thing about where you live?
Less traffic than Los Angeles, and it is the center of the tech industry.

How has life changed in your country since you were a child?
A lot more expensive for average level of lifestyle. Also, a lot more homeless.

What has been the most important event in your country in your lifetime?
Tough decision. 9/11, Covid, and Trump being President.

How has your view of work changed over time?
Tough to save money, as wages haven't kept up with inflation.

Tell me about your family:
Married to daughter of Chinese immigrants, with two kids (one boy and one girl), both adopted from China.

What is the most important lesson that your family taught you?
To believe in God, and to be honest in your dealings.

What's your biggest fear?
Not having resources to retire on.

What is your greatest pride?
That I have been able to see a lot of the world first-hand.

What was the favorite time of your life?
When I was living in Russia during its early changes, and then seeing China and Asia change over 25 years.

What is the best decision you made?
To live in Russia for a while in 1993, and to move to Asia in 1995 (where I stayed for over 25 years in Hong Kong and China).

Do you have a hidden talent?
Connecting with people.

What advice do you have for the next generation?
You become less anxious about some things as you get older. A song I like to think of, too, is called "Dear Younger Me."

United States

William Nganje

Place of Birth:
Buea, Cameroon

Current Residence:
Fargo, North Dakota, United States

question and several individuals stop to help you. This is very refreshing as a black person.

How has life changed in your country since you were a child?

Not much. Most of Cameroon's infrastructure has declined and a significant amount of the population still lacks basic necessities like potable water and electricity. Plus, there has been war and fighting in the Anglophone region of Cameroon for almost a decade now.

What has been the most important event in your country in your lifetime?

The discovery of oil and natural gas. Cameroon also has several other natural resources and is a top producer of agricultural commodities.

How has your view of work changed over time?

It is the same. I go for excellence in the things I do. I don't take anything for granted.

Tell me about your family:

I have been married for 33 years with four children, one adopted child and two grandkids. The last son has a bachelor's degree in finance. The last daughter is a doctor of pharmacy like her mother. My first daughter has a nursing degree, my eldest sons have finance and health

What is the best thing about where you live?

The majority of people are loving in Fargo. They make you feel welcome and at home. I remember several instances when you ask a question and several individuals stop to help you. You're most happy when you help others.

What is the most important lesson that your family taught you?

Love each other and be there for others. You're most happy when you help others.

What's your biggest fear?

Poor health. As we get older, we have to constantly eat well and exercise.

What is your greatest pride?

Several research and teaching awards at the university and in the United States. Our kids and grandchildren are our biggest pride.

What was the favorite time of your life?

Now and always. I enjoy hard work. It is rewarding.

What is the best decision you made?

Getting married in my 20s. Marriage and children help you to become a man fast. It also helps you not to procrastinate. Lives now depend on you as a married person.

Do you have a hidden talent?

Dancing and sports. I have four gold medals in wrestling and ping pong from back in my university days.

What advice do you have for the next generation?

Work hard and go for excellence. Make the world a better place by helping others.

backgrounds. The oldest has a master's in public health and a bachelor's in nursing.

United States

Anthony Gleich

Place of Birth:
Columbus, Ohio, United States

Current Residence:
Chandler, Arizona, United States

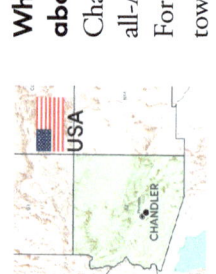

What is the best thing about where you live?

Chandler has been voted an all-American town twice. For a big city, it has a small-town vibe. My children graduated from high school here and we have many friends. We have easy access to all the cities around Phoenix.

How has life changed in your country since you were a child?

Growing up in the '70s and '80s, and becoming a legal adult, we understood what it was to live without all the technologies we currently have. Family was much more important. Values, morals, and just being good were sought after. We were raised to be patriotic and look out for one another.

What was the most important event in your country in your lifetime?

9/11 was the most impactful event — the attack on American soil and the uncertainty of that morning. My kids were in Head Start at the time. The country came together and was united. Who knew what the future held? Now I have two grandchildren who are 4 months old and who knows what to expect today? We have to continue with faith that good will prevail.

How has your view of work changed over time?

The attitude of self-gratification has prevailed. It seems that there is less concern for God, neighbor, and country. Greed leads so many.

The American dream and freedom are centered on life, liberty, and the pursuit of happiness, concepts that are not discerned nor sought after any longer. We need to seek to be humble.

Tell me about your family:

Venessa and I have been a couple for 38 years and married for 34. We have two children that are both adults now, and two new grandsons who are identical twins. There is nothing more important or valuable to me than my immediate family. Blessings abound and continue.

What is the most important lesson that your family taught you?

F.A.M.I.L.Y. Forget about me, I love you.

Love is self-sacrifice. I do not regret anything I have had to give up personally for the benefit of my wife, kids, and grandchildren. My reward is in witnessing their happiness.

What's your biggest fear?

Fear is not an emotion I choose to acknowledge. We have choices in every moment. I am an optimist who always fights for the good of all.

What is your greatest pride?

Pride is No. 1 of the seven deadly sins. My love grows more and more for my children. They have become loving, caring adults. This is my greatest joy.

What was the favorite time of your life?

When Venessa and I were in our first 10 years of marriage. There was the desire to build a good life for her and the kids. There are no guarantees. It is faith that has carried me through and has continued to give me hope.

What is the best decision you made?

Choosing Venessa to be my life partner.

Do you have a hidden talent?

I have always been an artist through drawing, which has led to many creative expressive actions such as a musician, songwriter, and ministry. These are the passions I long to pursue, and basic needs consume my time.

What advice do you have for future generations?

Slow down and look for the beauty in life. Do not take for granted anything and learn to have an attitude of gratitude. Do not forget that you did not choose your creation and that means that our lives are a gift with purpose. We have been created for the community, so let love lead the way.

AGRICULTURE NEAR CHANDLER, ARIZONA, UNITED STATES

CHRISTOPHER HARRIS/ISTOCKPHOTO

United States

Eric Knutson

Place of Birth:
Phoenix, Arizona, United States

Current Residence:
Gilbert, Arizona, United States

What is the best thing about where you live?

It would have to be the weather. It is beautiful nine months out of the year. I used to love everything about the Phoenix valley, but the rise in population in the last 10 years has really changed the dynamic of the people here.

How has life changed in your country since you were a child?

My country has changed quite a lot since I was a child. Life used to be about family and respect, and now it is about the individual — and selfishness.

What was the most important event in your country in your lifetime?

In my opinion, it would have to be the introduction of the internet. It has changed everything, and not always for the better.

How has your view of work changed over time?

My view of work has not changed. I still believe the more work you put into anything, the more benefit you receive from that work. My view of other people's work ethic has changed a lot.

Tell me about your family:

I grew up in a large family, with five older sisters. Mom and Dad were married for 55 years (before he passed). Now the family has grown to about 50 persons all living in or near the Phoenix valley. Christmas gatherings are a big deal — and sometimes impossible.

What is the most important lesson that your family taught you?

What I learned from my family is, let them have their own lives. Don't butt in too much. But know they are there for you in a pinch, or a catastrophe.

What's your biggest fear?

My biggest fear in life is realizing all my hard work with Flotsam and Jetsam will amount to nothing.

What is your greatest pride?

My greatest pride is, of course, my children. They have grown to be good human beings. They care for others and have strong values.

What was the favorite time of your life?

I think it would be the 1980s and 1990s, touring the world as an entertainer or raising my kids. Both times are very special to me.

What is the best decision you made?

Marrying my wife and loving my children unconditionally.

Do you have a hidden talent?

Not very hidden is the list of my talents. I can sing better than most, I can build a house from the ground up, myself. I can drive or operate almost anything with a motor and controls (including most aircraft). I can survive in the woods with nothing but a knife, indefinitely. I am a decent natural actor. And I am an extremely good whistler.

What advice do you have for future generations?

Keep an eye out for the consequences of your actions, before you act. Be loving and tolerant of all, the best you can. Don't sweat the small stuff; work them out quickly to the benefit of all and move on. Life is short.

SUPERSTITION MOUNTAINS NEAR PHOENIX, ARIZONA, UNITED STATES

NADER ABUSHHAB/UNSPLASH

Canada

Zvi Leve

Place of Birth:
New York City, New York, United States

Current Residence:
Montréal, Québec, Canada

What is the best thing about where you live?
I love the attitude about streets as public space.

How has life changed in your country since you were a child?
I only moved here when I was 30 years old (after living almost a decade in Israel), so it's hard to say but I do know quite a bit about Québec history. Québec had a *révolution tranquille* (a "quiet revolution") in the 1960s when the influence of the Catholic Church was expunged from all elements of Québec society and there was profound social change.

The rise of Québec nationalism (and other economic and transportation factors) led to significant disinvestment and a large population exodus from Montréal from the 1980s up until the early 2000s. Many people in the "anglophone" community (which absorbed non-Catholic immigrants) left Montréal, but I have no problem "Living in French," as the government says.

What has been the most important event in your country in your lifetime?
That would probably be the 1995 referendum in Québec to separate from Canada, which happened just a few months after I arrived here! The results were essentially 50/50 and Québec has been going its own way ever since. The "Maple Spring," which began as a student protest about tuition increases in 2012, eventually evolved into a broad-based social movement that brought down the government, which was also impressive.

How has your view of work changed over time?
Much of my life experience has been in precarious economic times so I have never felt a strong association between one's "work" and one's "sense of self." One of the things that I love the most about Montréal is that people here tend to have a very healthy work-life balance: they work enough so that they can live, but their lives are not defined by their work.

Tell me about your family:
Family can mean so many things! Beyond my two children, who are now young adults, I am not particularly close with my "biological" family. I think that one of the reasons why I fell in love with my ex was because she had such a tight-knit family. Ironically, it was in some ways her struggles with her own family that spilled over a bit into our own relationship. In any case, I have no regrets — it is thanks to her that I live in Montréal and we have raised two wonderful children together.

What is the most important lesson that your family taught you?
Patience.

What's your biggest fear?
I am not afraid of much, but I suppose that I fear being around to witness the "end of the world" as we know it. It saddens me to think that my children will likely be confronted with the fallout of our own inability to change — disruptive change and uncertainty will become the new normal. I do not expect humankind to go out with a bang, but rather we will be grappling for

the foreseeable future with a prolonged period of worsening economic and environmental conditions punctuated perhaps with sporadic episodes of violence and social dislocations.

What is your greatest pride?
That I have raised two very sensitive and thoughtful kids.

What was the favorite time of your life?
I always try to make the most of the present moment so I do not dwell much on the past. I have traveled quite a bit (mostly for work), and some of my trips were wonderful adventures. Now I do my "road trips" mostly by bicycle, and I am having a wonderful time going on short outings with my partner and one or the other of my kids.

What is the best decision you made?
To move to Montréal.

Do you have a hidden talent?
Apparently, I pick up languages quite quickly.

What advice do you have for the next generation?
Be flexible and think for yourselves.

social media has spilled over into using the same rude manner of speech in person.

What has been the most important event in your country in your lifetime?

One was the 150th anniversary of the Confederation of Canada in 2017, a year-long celebration of all things Canadian: from basketball, lacrosse, and ice hockey to maple syrup everything; from our awesome national parks to the Canadian National Railway (unfortunately a sad shadow of its former self). Most people found something worth celebrating, remembering, and treasuring.

How has your view of work changed over time?

My opinion about, and attitude toward, work has evolved since I had my first job delivering the *Toronto Star* daily newspaper in 1976. It was only a six-day-a-week paper at that time, so Sunday was truly a day of rest.

But I learned to love the accomplishment of it all: the efficiency of "threading" the sections of the paper together prior to delivery; meeting the customers along the way and on every Saturday while collecting the money for subscriptions; the balance and strength needed to ride a bicycle while loaded with Saturday papers in two carrying bags slung over my shoulders; and the pocket money!

Although my main occupation was an English teacher in high schools for 32 years (including a teaching exchange in Australia in 2012), I've worked as a landscaper, a back-country canoe trip outfitter, a chicken wrangler for a day, a tea factory hand for a day, a food and alcohol delivery driver, a

What is the best thing about where you live?

There is a lot to like about Utopia: the distinct four seasons; a rural setting close enough to a city of 150,000 for "nightlife" but far enough to get away from most of the light pollution and traffic congestion. Our 1.6-acre property gives purpose and beauty to my life, as well as having great neighbors and ease of access to cycling routes.

How has life changed in your country since you were a child?

Ontario — and Canada, for that matter — has undergone many changes since I was a child: many for the good, some not so much.

Honda Manufacturing moved to Alliston before I finished high school in the early 1980s and brought a prosperity that was missing from the town, as well as a demand for different foods at the local grocery stores. Unfortunately, that plant gobbled up a lot of prime farmland, as have the housing developments built since then.

Having said that, Essa township, which contains Utopia, is a region of rolling hills and more than a few gravel roads (still!). It is still quite agrarian, economically, and very friendly.

Politically, the nature of discourse is ugly — something that is quite sad, historically speaking. The polar extremes of the parties and their supporters make conversation with a stranger a minefield. Even a decade ago, that was not the case, and I think that the perceived anonymity of

Canada
Vince Filo-Carroll

Place of Birth:
Alliston, Ontario, Canada

Current Residence:
Utopia, Ontario, Canada
(about 30 kilometers north of Alliston!)

bartender, a DJ, a night-shift grocery stock clerk, a soccer referee — and those were just the paid gigs.

In summary, what I've learned is the following: Don't be afraid to work hard; use the tools you have; borrow (and return!) the tools you need; ask questions; and show some initiative.

Tell me about your family:

I am married to Marian, the first and only, for 35 years now, and we have two amazing children: Tyler, following in his parents' footsteps as a high school teacher, and forging his own path as a fiction writer; and a daughter, Tara, who is not content with merely graduating with a degree in sports and physical education but is also pursuing a paramedicine certification. Both are strong, beautiful people.

What is the most important lesson your family taught you?

The main one from both our families is about tradition and pride in one's culture. Both of my parents came from Derry in Northern Ireland and emigrated to Canada in July of 1961; the day after they got married, they sailed to Montreal on the Saxonia. But Ireland never really left them. A soft Irish accent could always be heard in my mother's voice, right up to her final days in 2021. Irish music, both folk and operatic Irish tenors or sopranos, was the first music I remember hearing. Irish whiskey was my father's drink of choice, as is mine. On the Carroll family trip to Ireland in 1975 — the only trip abroad the family ever took — everywhere we visited there was always singing involved, and always lots of shared hugs and the warmth.

What's your biggest fear?

Fears are definitely things that, when I was growing up, one did not address or talk about. The strong were silent, one strove not to bring shame upon the family, and heaven help you if you did! But it seems to me that today, it has more to do with my children than myself.

The reality is that, to develop as a whole adult, one must come to know and understand that geography, and develop skills to deal with it. Not to spend a lot of time there, but to recognize that resilience is grown from it. It speaks to one of my favorite quotations I used to use as a writing assignment: "There are only two things we can bequeath to our children: roots and wings."

What is your greatest pride?

Of all that I've accomplished so far, my two children fill me with so much pride and emotion. And I let them know that, not to put pressure on them, but as a way of saying, "Keep going, there's so much more you'll discover and accomplish, and I'll be there supporting you every step of the way!"

What was the favorite part of your life?

The urge for nostalgia is strong but I have to say that the favorite time in my life is now, the present. Everything has led to this point in my life: my upbringing, my relationships, and my experiences are always informing each day, and help me discern meaning in whatever I do.

What is the best decision you made?

Decisions, and the process of making the really big ones, like buying cars or houses, going on really long trips, or choosing a life partner, have so many dimensions to consider. Sometimes the crystal ball one peers into shows a pretty rosy future; sometimes the image is grainy or a bit out of focus, but the overall color is promising something rewarding. And often decisions require commitments, and follow-through. But the best decision I have ever made is to marry Marian. For almost 40 years, all of the highlights in my life have involved Marian in some way.

Do you have a hidden talent?

A hidden talent for me would be one that I'm either shy about revealing or developing, like drawing or cooking. But cooking is coming along!

What advice do you have for the next generation?

Do not bottle up frustrations and anxieties. Let off a healthy dose of steam on a regular basis, either by doing something you love or by talking it out with someone you trust, or writing it out — but not on social media. As well, get involved as a volunteer with a movement or non-profit agency that you believe in. But whatever else you do, commit to living fully!

EDITOR'S NOTE: *Vince Filo-Carroll sadly passed away on July 20, 2024. He was a thoughtful gentleman who showed great interest in this project. Rest in peace, my friend.*

Canada

John McPhee

Place of Birth:
Hamilton, Canada, but I grew up in Cape Breton, Canada. (I will always be a Cape Bretoner at heart.)

Current Residence:
Waterloo, Ontario, Canada

What is the best thing about where you live?

1. Easy access to the outdoors and (mostly) clean air and water.
2. Many golf courses and hockey rinks.
3. Two universities and a wide variety of restaurants.

How has life changed in your country since you were a child?

1. It has become very hard to maintain an outdoor ice rink for more than a few days in winter due to climate change.
2. Social skills have deteriorated, likely due to cellphones and the Covid-19 pandemic.
3. Politicians are much more concerned with the next election and party lines than long-term improvements to the country.

What has been the most important event in your country in your lifetime?

The Covid-19 pandemic.

How has your view of work changed over time?

It is less stressful and more enjoyable as I get closer to retirement. I am fortunate to work with young, smart, and curious students who continue to educate me.

Tell me about your family:

One wife, three children. My wife is a super-smart engineer and a great mother. Three very different and successful children.

What is the most important lesson that your family taught you?

It's okay to stop and smell the roses.

What's your biggest fear?

Harm to my children.

What is your greatest pride?

My children.

What was the favorite time of your life?

1. Graduate student in university in my 20s. Little income, but tons of freedom to explore new ideas, relationships, and the outdoors.
2. Right now. I'm healthy, active in hockey and golf, financially secure, challenged at work (still), and have a great family.

What is the best decision you made?

Marrying my wife.

Do you have a hidden talent?

Pattern recognition, e.g. a typo on a printed page full of text will leap out at me before I read a single word. It's weird.

What advice do you have for the next generation?

Put your cellphones away and read a printed book. Any book. It will stimulate your brain.

Mexico

Rene Gastelum Campoy

Place of Birth:
Ciudad Obregón, Sonora, Mexico

Current Residence:
Ciudad Obregón, Sonora, Mexico

What is the best thing about where you live?

I live in a city of 400,000 inhabitants that has wide streets, a very square design that allows for very easy and safe vehicular traffic, which allows us to move very easily and in a short time. The population is mostly native people who preserve their traditions, are very affectionate and who are welcoming. It is a city that has mountains, beaches and a desert in its surroundings. Our climate, despite being hot in the summer, allows you to enjoy these attractions year-round. And the best is saved for last — our food! We have the best seafood and meat in the world!

How has life changed in your country since you were a child?

In the last 50 years, life has changed a lot in my country, for better and for worse. For the better, today we have more comforts at home, better transportation, better health services, better access to quality education, and more access to cultural, artistic and sporting events. There is more acceptance and openness to different ways of thinking about topics such as politics, sexual preference, music, clothing and coexistence.

But today, children no longer live life together, playing in the streets and parks. They are inside their house, isolating themselves with their electronic games. Families are dispersed; there is no longer respect for the elderly, women, or children. There is access to drugs, a loss of values, an increase in violence, corruption in governments and society, and impunity in the application of justice.

What has been the most important event in your country in your lifetime?

The restoration of democracy in politics in the 1990s, and all the evils that the drug trafficking business brought with it.

How has your view of work changed over time?

Before, it was enough to work long and hard to have success. Interpersonal relationships were fundamental; problems and stress were of a smaller scale with smaller consequences. Nowadays everything revolves around technology. You have to be trained and keep up-to-date with so many evolutions to be able to stay and advance. The decrease in values and ethics makes the operation and administration of companies more difficult.

Tell me about your family:

I have eight brothers and a lot of nephews with whom I have lived all my life, always very united and happy. We really like to get together under any pretext. I am married with three adorable daughters, who are already professionals and single. I have a very hardworking wife with a very big and special heart and spirit.

What is the most important lesson that your family taught you?

Union, love and family coexistence are the pillars to allow you to aspire and to grow and be.

What's your biggest fear?

Not achieving my dreams and happiness.

What is your greatest pride?

My family and my work.

What was the favorite time of your life?

My youth. There were few (and insignificant) worries, I was always living day to day with family and friends, and I was full of dreams, health and energy.

What is the best decision you made?

Life put me in very difficult and painful situations. Overcoming them, despite the adversities, has been the most difficult thing I have ever experienced. But it was the best path I could have taken.

Do you have a hidden talent?

I believe that we all have hidden talents. There are those who find and develop one or more, there are those who do not find them, and there are those who do not even look for them.

What advice do you have for the next generation?

Recover and preserve through their use and teachings the fundamental values and traditions of the family and society.

Mexico

Juan Gabriel Guerra

Place of Birth:
León, Mexico

Current Residence:
Cancún, Mexico

What is the best thing about where you live?
The beaches and coral reefs.

How has life changed in your country since you were a child?
Unfortunately, my country has changed with more insecurity and poverty. The political spectrum doesn't look good, either.

What has been the most important event in your country in your lifetime?
It was the 1986 earthquake, which killed thousands of people in Mexico City and destroyed hundreds of buildings. The most important event in *my* life is probably when I got ordained Catholic priest at the Vatican by John Paul II.

How has your view of work changed over time?
My vision of work is that it is the best way to develop as a person and that loving what you do is the key to being happy.

What is the most important thing your family taught you?
A love of nature and outdoor activities, and that to achieve your goals, you have to work and be responsible, kind and have respect for others.

What is your biggest fear?
Losing my position as a priest.

What is your greatest pride?
It is that I persevered until now serving as a priest

What was the favorite time of my life?
My favorite moment was when I carried out a mission with *The Passion of the Christ* actor Jim Caviezel in the city of Las Montañas de Veracruz, Mexico.

What is the best decision you made?
To be a priest.

Do you have a hidden talent?
I don't feel like I have any hidden talent.

What advice do you have for the next generation?
To fight for what is right, despite the contrary opinion of the majority; fight for personal values and convictions. Do not exclude God from your life and respect The Decalogue (The 10 Commandments).

BERMUDA

SINT MAARTEN

ARUBA

PANAMA

COLOMBIA

ECUADOR

BRAZIL

ARGENTINA

CHILE

THE CARIBBEAN, CENTRAL AMERICA, AND SOUTH AMERICA

IF NORTH AMERICA IN THE LAST 60 YEARS WAS MARKED BY
STABILITY, THE COUNTRIES OF THE CARIBBEAN, CENTRAL AMERICA,
AND SOUTH AMERICA WERE THE OPPOSITE — EXPERIENCING ALL
TYPES OF GOVERNANCE AND LEADERS SINCE THE 1960S.

FIRST, like on other continents, former colonies of Great Britain, the Netherlands, and France gained independence after World War II or, in some cases, chose to stay aligned with their "home" country. This created a vacuum to be filled with various forms of government and representation, which led to. . .

Second, the aggressiveness of communist influences to gain footholds in the Western Hemisphere, with the backing of the Soviet Union and its satellites. This, as expected, provoked meddling in those nations' domestic politics by Western countries, with subsequent violence, guerrilla warfare, insurgencies, and inconsistent application of those nations' laws by the ruling party.

Third, economic issues — like unemployment, worker conditions, government spending, corruption, tariffs on imports, and currency valuations — provided all sorts of sparks to ignite coups, military takeovers and revolutions.

In some of the biggest countries — Brazil, Argentina, Peru, and Chile — attempts at creating democratic republics were thwarted in the 1960s by military juntas acting to protect the nation against socialists and leftists with different objectives. As social order disintegrated, a pendulum swung for law and order, which inevitably led to abuses and reduced rights for the governed. The left wing fought the right wing, then the right wing fought the left wing. This dominated

South American nations until the mid-1980s, when an emphasis on trade, manufacturing, and exports provided glimmers of a different future.

Citizens in the smaller countries of Central America experienced a similar roller-coaster but often with greater extremes, due to the close proximity of all of the participants (and their allies in neighboring countries).

Since the turn of the 21st century, the area — with the exception of Venezuela — has been relatively peaceful, except in countries involved in the ever-present drug trade. Citizens have felt more empowered and protests have led to change — and fewer violent purges

Bermuda
Dennis Cherry

Place of Birth:
Paget, Bermuda

Current Residence:
Hamilton Parish, Bermuda

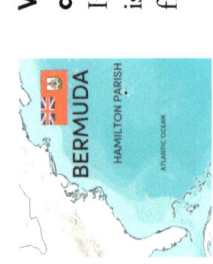

What is the best thing about where you live?
It's a beautiful, safe island with unique, friendly people.

How has life changed in your country since you were a child?
Being born and growing up in Bermuda was awesome. Now everything is faster, more aggressive, and less about community.

What has been the most important event in your country in your lifetime?
The Covid-19 pandemic.

How has your view of work changed over time?
I was born in Bermuda and lived in Sandy's Parish with my parents and sister. As a youth I played cricket, football, rugby, sailed and swam, as well as owning and riding ponies and later horses in competitions.

As a teen I found the island quite small and limiting one's opportunities, in regard to competing in equestrian events. I used to compete in Ontario, Canada for the summer holiday and was part of the Young Riders' Bermuda team in the three-day event: dressage, cross country and stadium-jumping.

I finished my school exams at 17. I returned during the winter months in order to work on houses (painting and carpentry) and bartending at night at a local Italian restaurant. Then I would tend bar at a nightclub afterwards, until the early morning.

After my 1992 Olympic campaign came to an unhappy end, I returned to the island and started a small carpentry business, which grew into a construction business. I then took over an importation and supply company, which purchases products online for our customers, which we deliver and sometimes assemble as well. Over the years our cost-of-living in Bermuda has increased so much. I now work seven days a week — every week.

Tell me about your family:
I am married to an awesome lady. We have three lovely children, a son, 17, and twins, 14. My mother and sister (and nieces and a nephew) live on the island. My father recently passed away.

My in-laws also live on the island. My mother in-law is from England and my father-in-law is from the United States. I have a lot of friends worldwide.

What is the most important lesson that your family taught you?
Honesty and integrity, without question.

What's your biggest fear?
Heights. My country's well-being. Closed-in spaces.

What is your greatest pride?
My honesty and my family.

What was the favorite time of your life?
This one.

FRONT STREET, HAMILTON, BERMUDA
KINO/UNSPLASH

What is the best decision you made?
Marrying my wifey.

Do you have a hidden talent?
No, I do not hide much.

What advice do you have for the next generation?
Work hard! Pay attention. Have fun and laugh. Be safe and be honest!

Sint Maarten

Juan Pablo M. Piscione

Place of Birth:
Buenos Aires, Argentina

Current Residence:
Sint Maarten/St. Martin

What is the best thing about where you live?
The freedom and the ocean surrounding the island.

How has life changed in your country since you were a child?
I would not know as I have not returned there in 10 years.

What has been the most important event in your country in your lifetime?
World Cup champions three times!

How has your view of work changed over time?
The world has gotten smaller with the ease of traveling and making international interactions. Communication via the World Wide Web has made this possible.

Tell me about your family:
I married a Sint Maartener and we conceived two bright boys with ample and broad views of the world.

What is the most important lesson that your family taught you?
Be open-minded. The one thing that surely helped was the blessed opportunity to travel from a young age.

What's your biggest fear?
I don't know and I'm not sure I want to think hard about it.

What is your greatest pride?
The family that I have formed.

What was the favorite time of your life?
The present.

What is the best decision you made?
Settling on Sint Maarten.

Do you have a hidden talent?
Waterman.

What advice do you have for the next generation?
Live every minute and learn to disengage from social media and virtual experiences. Instead, touch and feel this beautiful planet we have been given.

Aruba

Francisco Javier Gonzalez

Place of Birth:
Aruba

Current Residence:
Hooiberg, Aruba

What is the best thing about where you live?
Safety and being a Dutch colony.

How has life changed in your country since you were a child?
Prosperity, through the oil refinery and tourism.

What has been the most important event in your country in your lifetime?
The decision to stay a Dutch colony in 1986.

How has your view of work changed over time?
In accounting, same as around the world, it is all of the digitalizing.

What is the most important lesson that your family taught you?
Hard work, honesty, and to be grateful.

What's your biggest fear?
People's stupidity.

What is your greatest pride?
My daughter.

What was the favorite time of your life?
Each time to enjoy as it comes.

What is the best decision you made?
Marrying my wife.

STATUE OF ANNE FRANK, ORANJESTAD, ARUBA

PHOTO BY THE AUTHOR

Do you have a hidden talent?
Not that I know of (it's too hidden).

What advice do you have for the next generation?
Study, read, know world history, and learn from past mistakes.

Panama

Jaime Roberto Robleto Aguilar

Place of Birth:
Panama City, Panama

Current Residence:
I live in a "country area" named Nuevo Arraijan, 13 miles west of Panama City, Panama.

What is the best thing about where you live?

This area grew a series of neighborhoods with streets, green areas, health centers, potable water, electricity, and public transportation (contrary to what happened in other places nearby).

Panama is small, with close to 4 million souls; all of us have come from elsewhere, and we have learned to respect each other and to get along well. For example, here you will see the pastor, the rabbi, the priest, and the monk enjoying a cup of coffee. It is not a surprise to see interracial couples. The wealthy people, the middle class, and the poor visit shopping malls and parks and no one cares about it.

How has life changed in your country since you were a child?

To my mind, the most important one is that most people understand that women have the potential to do more than housekeeping. As a result, if you take a look at the education statistics, it's normal that women have better grades than men and among the three best students, usually the top one is female. Women have gone well beyond their "traditional role" and do not depend on a male to survive.

What has been the most important event in your country in your lifetime?

No doubt, it was Panamanian people operating the canal, beginning on Dec. 31, 1999. We have pride that, with all due respect, we have done it

better than the Americans, to show that we have the skills and will necessary to be successful.

How has your view of work changed over time?

Way back you dreamed to be a teacher. You studied, you got your degree, you were hired as a teacher and, after many years, you retired. However, today you study one thing, most probably you'll be working in another thing, and you will be moving from one company to another or opening your own business.

Tell me about your family:

Down here men were expected to be gentlemen, so, before having a girlfriend or a formal relationship, one must get a permanent source of income. For that reason, I married at 33 years old, tried to do my best for my family, put bread on the table, helped with housekeeping and spent as much time with my wife and kids, until one day I realized that she didn't care about me. After hard years, I'm starting a new relationship. In the end, I learned that love isn't a feeling, it's a decision. I also learned that when both people want something, it's possible to overcome everything.

What is your biggest fear?

Politicians, who just want power to get money, and the ignorants who still believe in them.

What is your greatest pride?

I always have tried to do good to others, though I'm not perfect. When I fall in disgrace, many people help me (thank God for them).

What was the favorite time of your life?
When I thought that I had a perfect
family. (Sorry, but it is the truth.)

What is the best decision you made?
To think about my wellbeing.

Do you have a hidden talent?
Patience.

**What advice do you have for
the next generation?**
Educate yourself, think, and enjoy every day as if
it is your last. Don't live to work and work to live
because it will take you to nowhere.

Colombia

Jorge Armando Duran Castano

Place of Birth:
Bogotá, Colombia

Current Residence:
Bogotá, Colombia

What is the best thing about where you live?
The people.

How has life changed in your country since you were a child?
Drug trafficking permeates the values of society.

What has been the most important event in your country in your lifetime?
The preservation of democracy until now.

How has your view of work changed over time?
Every day is more technical but more metallic.

What is the most important lesson that your family taught you?
Honesty and work.

What's your biggest fear?
Not having my health.

What is your greatest pride?
My family.

What was the favorite time of your life?
Birth of my children.

What is the best decision you made?
Marrying my wife.

Do you have a hidden talent?
Yes, I write.

What advice do you have for the next generation?
Don't abandon the simple values of life.

Colombia

Mauricio Rodriguez

Place of Birth:
Bogotá, Colombia

Current Residence:
Bogotá, Colombia

What is the best thing about where you live?
My friends and family that live here. About the city, it is the climate, cultural life and natural environment.

What's your biggest fear?
A prolonged and painful sickness.

How has life changed in your country since you were a child?
Lots of economic and social progress but we still have serious problems with violence, inequality and corruption.

What has been the most important event in your country in your lifetime?
The peace agreement signed with the FARC guerrilla group in 2016.

How has your view of work changed over time?
Work must be intellectually satisfying and not just a source of income. And we must have enough time left for our family and friends, and for our hobbies and for rest.

Tell me about your family:
Wonderful parents (may they rest in peace), six wonderful sisters and one wonderful brother. Two wonderful sons from my first marriage, one wonderful daughter from my second marriage. I'm happily married to my wonderful second wife.

What is the most important lesson that your family taught you?
The value of integrity, discipline, and solidarity.

What is your greatest pride?
My wonderful sons and daughter.

What was the favorite time of your life?
My answer, over the years, is always the same: Now.

What is the best decision you made?
Marrying my two wonderful wives, with whom we raised three wonderful children.

Do you have a hidden talent?
I don't think so, but you never know. . . .

What advice do you have for the next generation?
Carpe diem — Seize the day! Enjoy every moment, and don't be a slave of your past or a prisoner of your future.

Ecuador

Francisco Guayasamin

Place of Birth:
Quito, Ecuador

Current Residence:
Quito, Ecuador

What is the best thing about where you live?

I live in the "middle of the world" along the Equator, so what I love the most is the weather. In Quito we only have two seasons: rainy and dry. But the weather is like the same all the time. So we don't need to have heaters or air conditioning in our house.

With this weather, we can produce all kinds of vegetables and fruits year-round. That is why food here is cheap. You can get a bunch of bananas for $1.00, for example.

Also, time is equal — always sunrise at 6 a.m. and sunset at 6 p.m. It never changes. We can change our weather very fast. If we want snow, we can go to the snowcapped mountains in few minutes, or we can go to the jungle or to the beach. Ecuador is very diverse. We are pluricultural and multiethnic. In a small like country ours — the size of the state of Colorado — we have a lot of diversity.

How has life changed in your country since you were a child?

Everything has changed around the world, especially in Latin America.

Ecuador used to be very Catholic, conservative and with machismo. Things are changing because of technology. Young people can get a lot of information today.

There is more respect for diversity. Before we used to have a lot of discrimination. The problem is that people don't like to read, so education is getting worse, with little substance about history

and culture. People here know more about *fútbol* (soccer) than the history of the political situation of the country.

What has been the most important event in your country in your lifetime?

For me as a gay man, since 1998 in our constitution we are no longer considered criminals and since 2008 it is forbidden to discriminate in Ecuador for any kind of reason.

Life has become easier for us. Before we used to have a lot of persecution, people in jail, and also saw a lot of young guys commit suicide.

How has your view of work changed over time?

In my country it always has been very difficult to get a good job. That is one of the biggest problems.

I love my country but the politicians here are awful. They stole a lot of money from the people, so education, health and culture are not supported in my country. It is very difficult to get a job or start your own business. Corruption continues in a lot of government departments.

Ecuador has a lot of bureaucracy. A lot of people are preferring to go find new opportunities, especially in the United States and some countries in Europe.

I love my job but I don't have customers every moment. I also don't have any social security and the public health system is bad. So my life is like a miracle: surviving every day, as many Ecuadorians do.

Tell me about your family:

I was raised with an adoptive family until I was 23. I didn't have any good experiences with them. I haven't seen them since I left.

Since then I have lived alone. I have a great family of 10 cats and five dogs. All of them were rescued.

What's your biggest fear?

Getting sick in this country.

What is your greatest pride?

I did a lot of great things by myself. I became a gay activist and I did a lot of actions that helped make Ecuador a country with less discrimination. Also, I love my job. I work as a tour guide for gay people who want to know my country.

Do you have a hidden talent?

I love writing. I wrote a book, *Bienvenido al Mundo de las Apariencias* (*Welcome to the World of Appearances*) and I write some articles at: franciscoguayasamin.blogspot.com.

What advice do you have for the next generation?

Learn about respect. First for yourself and then for others. If we don't respect the diversity of life and our world, life will be a hell. And that is happening in a lot of places around the Earth.

adoptive parents — it is really helpful to go to a support group. It is one of the ways that I can leave the past behind and go forward.

What is the most important lesson that your family taught you?

I preferred to live very far from people who don't love me. I prefer to live alone.

I work as a volunteer with a lot of people whose parents don't love them. I teach them how to love themselves, how to rescue their dignity, and live apart from their parents. In that way, they can heal from a lot of pain that they have inside.

What was the favorite time of your life?

When I am working. I love guiding and traveling with my tourists.

What is the best decision you made?

To ask for help. When you are abused in so many ways by your parents — in my case, with my

Brazil

Marcos Netto

Place of Birth:
Canoas, Rio Grande do Sul, Brazil

Current Residence:
Canoas, Rio Grande do Sul, Brazil

What is the best thing about where you live?

The city is a big one (400,000 people). But I always feel like I am living in a small village because I know many people here.

So, it feels like a family. Besides that, the city is in a strategic part of southern Brazil, near the border of three countries. So, it makes it convenient to travel.

How has life changed in your country since you were a child?

Life seemed to be simpler and less complicated then. We could live without the technology and all the high-end gadgets we have today. Also, the country was not so dangerous.

What has been the most important event in your country in your lifetime?

That is tough to answer. But I'm sure it was the conviction of our former president to jail for a gigantic scheme of corruption, and his later release by the Supreme Court, which was composed of individuals appointed by him or his party. It was a scandal that will take its toll on the country for many generations to come.

How has your view of work changed over time?

Work remained the same over the years. What we have now is a new set of tools that are supposed to make workers more productive. There are also new quality and performance standards, which were nonexistent or non-used in the past. And today when someone is choosing a profession,

it is wise to think about the chances of becoming obsolete or being replaced by a machine in the future.

Tell me about your family:

I came from a traditional family. Born and raised Catholic from parents that remained married all their lives. Kinda followed the example and got married to a high school sweetheart and we are still together after 30 years. Our children (a boy and a girl) had all the influences and advice to become good persons and good citizens.

What is the most important lesson that your family taught you?

Family is the base of everything. Simple as that.

What's your biggest fear?

I don't think much about that. But I could say that I don't like much the idea of getting older and becoming a burden for some of my loved ones. I just hope I stay healthy and sane until the day I pass away.

What is your greatest pride?

My children! No doubt about that! They are everything I could wish for and more!

What was the favorite time of your life?

Back in 1984 I decided to "see the world." I embarked on a 12-month journey outside Brazil. In 1985 I visited North America and many countries in Europe. Got back with a feeling that I had lived and learned 10 years in one. That experience changed my life forever.

What is the best decision you made?

A few years ago I quit my boring work life as a director in a local company and decided to pursue my long-time dreams. I took courses in wine-tasting and tourism. Now I am a certified sommelier and tour guide. My job consists of bringing people to delicious experiences around Brazil. I wish I had done it before.

Do you have a hidden talent?

I have a special gift to learn new languages. Put me in a different country for a few weeks and I am communicating with them in no time!

What advice do you have for the next generation?

Be honest, work hard and never stop chasing your dreams. They will become a reality sooner or later.

Argentina

Dante Alfredo Rodriguez

Place of Birth:
Villa María, Province of Córdoba, Argentina

Current Residence:
Villa María, Province of Córdoba, Argentina

What is the best thing about where you live?

It is a city in the center of the country, one of the few where you can still have peace and security with great commercial and agricultural development.

How has life changed in your country since you were a child?

Argentina is a wonderful country, with all its diverse climates and very friendly and hard-working people. (I am only talking about ordinary people, not about politicians or powerful people.) There have been no major changes, only a military *coup d'état*, the unnecessary Malvinas War (also known as the Falklands War) and the governments constantly repeating themselves making the same mistakes; the other side is always chosen so that the one who is there leaves.

What has been the most important event in your country during your life?

The military coup of 1976 and the Malvinas War with the United Kingdom in 1982.

How has your view of work changed over time?

I always had — and many of us have — the work culture incorporated into us. There are parasitic people from the different governments but they are a minority. In general, we are workers.

Tell me about your family:

I lost my wife when I was young to cancer, and I had to raise my three children with a lot of sacrifice.

What is the most important lesson your family taught you?

I think the experience with my wife taught me to appreciate and know how to value the person you have as a life partner.

What's your biggest fear?

Reaching old age with some serious health problem and complicating the lives of my children.

What is your greatest pride?

Having been a good husband, a good father — a little upright perhaps — and having always been an outstanding worker in every place I worked.

What was the favorite time of your life?

The birth of my children.

What is the best decision you made?

My best decision was perhaps to make the financial sacrifice to be able to see places in the world when I grew up.

Do you have a hidden talent?

Hidden? No. I am a perfectionist in everything I do. I put passion into each task and that led me to always be in high demand where I was hired.

What advice do you have for the next generation?

Study, be good people and acquire intelligence so that you know how to protect yourself and never allow yourself to be devalued.

Chile

Andres Sanhueza

Place of Birth:
Santiago, Chile

Current Residence:
Coyhaique, Chile

What is the best thing about where you live?
It is the best location of Chilean Patagonia: nature, weather, lifestyle, outdoors, food and freedom.

Tell me about your family:
I'm divorced, have a 17-year-old daughter and I've been in a relationship the last four years. My daughter lives in Santiago with her mother and I live in Coyhaique with Vanessa.

What is the most important lesson that your family taught you?
If you choose to be a gardener, it is ok — but just be the *best gardener ever!* Follow your dreams but be the best at what you choose to do!

What's your biggest fear?
Uncertainty.

What is your greatest pride?
My daughter.

What was the favorite time of your life?
Living on Easter Island, personally and professionally speaking. (It is part of Chile but about 2,300 miles into the Pacific Ocean.)

What is the best decision you made?
Mostly when I make decisions in which my staff at any property is involved.

Do you have a hidden talent?
Not any really.

What advice do you have for the next generation?
Never, ever give up.

How has life changed in your country since you were a child?
Politically speaking I was born under a military government, which means some restrictions but overall we built a strong country in democracy, economics, and culture. When I turned 18 years old, the military government delivered the country to a democratically elected president.

Secondly, the Carretera Austral — a 1,700-kilometer scenic route — was built from the mid-1980s here in Patagonia. It has become the main attraction for domestic and international tourism.

What has been the most important event in your country in your lifetime?
The transition from a military government to a democratic one, with free elections making a strong country.

How has your view of work changed over time?
Today you lead with teamwork — sharing and receiving the experience of your staff, team leaders and management. The old days — with management telling you what to do and not giving you the chance to be heard — are over.

number crunching are easier, but at the same time many more mistakes are possible, as work became automatic, typing words and numbers with no thinking process involved, as most assume the computer will resolve their work on its own.

Tell me about your family:

We are a tightly knit family, with values. We work together and respect each other, appreciating everybody else's talents. We work together, and we play together, two different environments.

What is the most important lesson that your family taught you?

Union and respect for all is important.

What's your biggest fear?

Not understanding world affairs that could maybe affect our decision-making process, both family-wise and business-wise.

What is your greatest pride?

My family, two sons, their wives, one daughter and my grandchildren.

What was the favorite time of your life?

As I always say, I live in a permanent vacation, so that I enjoy thoroughly every day, the good days and the bad days, as I see them pass. My college days were my favorite time (so far), though today, looking back, I feel I wasted too much time.

What is the best decision you made?

I listened to my father's advice when he was alive.

What is the best thing about where you live?

I'm close to the vineyards. Wine is my passion.

How has life changed in your country since you were a child?

Long answer, summarized. When I was a child, it was possible to play soccer with your friends or ride your bike around freely, in the streets. TV was restricted, so that homework and street playing were the usual daily activities. Children respected their elders, especially their parents and teachers. Calling your girlfriend meant she had to be waiting by the phone for your call or having to say hello to her mother. Today, family life has become a scarce privilege.

What has been the most important event in your country in your lifetime?

If I may, I'll talk about Chile. I believe it was the *coup d'état* in 1973 and the later democratic election that terminated the dictatorial period. This gave way to a very prosperous era when GDP growth and development brought Chile to be an example to be followed for the world.

How has your view of work changed over time?

I remember my father complaining about how people spent too much time fiddling with their computers. When I started working, and obviously, when I went to school, there was no Excel or Word, which meant you did your work by hand, with a pen and paper. With time, mechanical work has become easier, project forecasts and

Chile

1. Daniel Picciotto

Place of Birth:
Bogotá, Colombia

Current Residence:
Santiago, Chile

Do you have a hidden talent?
I like to sing, but I will not do it in public (or, not *again*).

What advice do you have for the next generation?
It's scary, but I feel the coming generations, the younger ones, are concentrated on the wrong values, with no principles, no ethic, and, mostly, no discipline. There will be a day when we aren't around, and they will not be able to depend on their parents.

PASEO BANDERA, SANTIAGO, CHILE
KEVIN WASILEVSKI/UNSPLASH

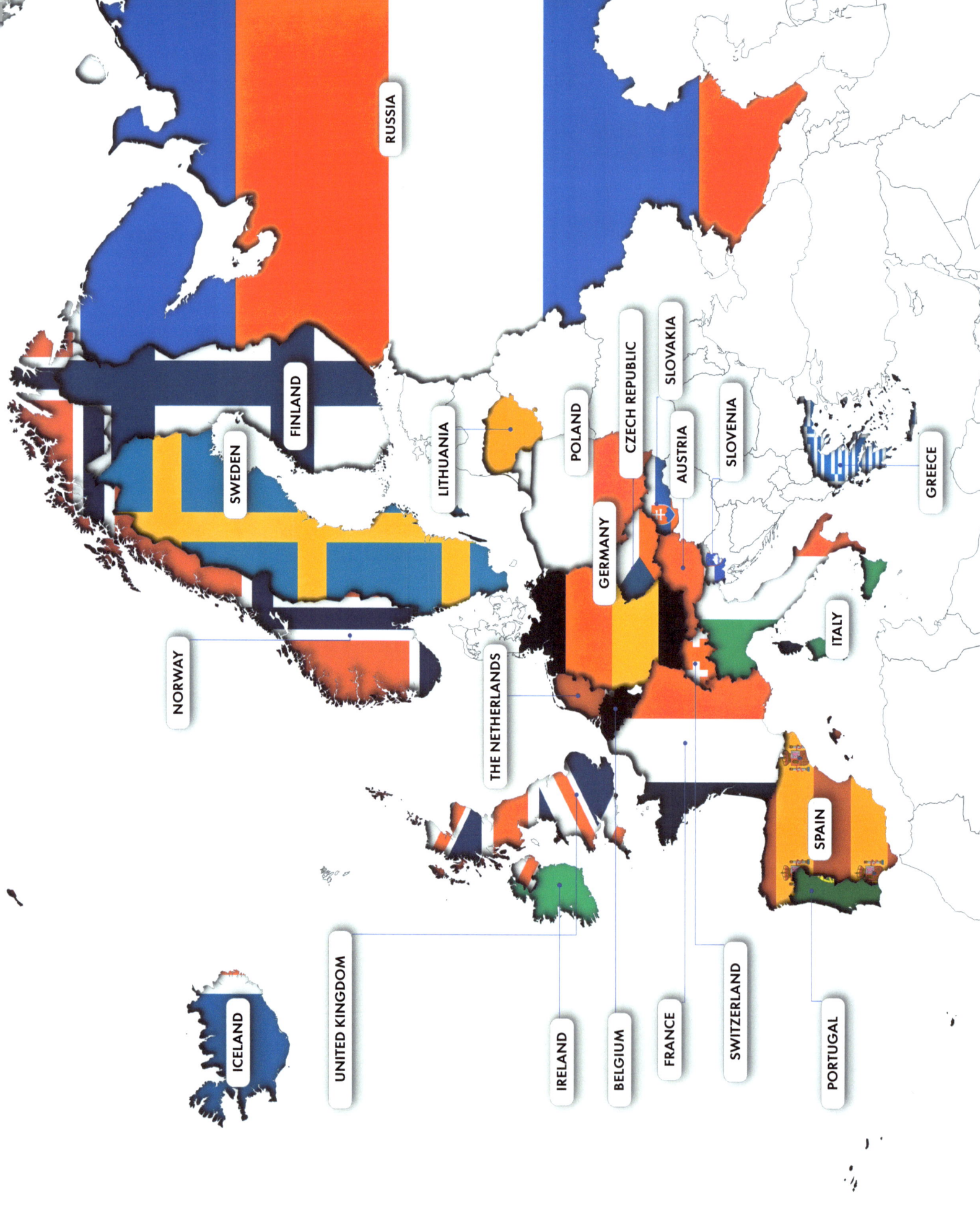

RUSSIA

FINLAND

SWEDEN

LITHUANIA

POLAND

CZECH REPUBLIC

SLOVAKIA

AUSTRIA

SLOVENIA

GREECE

NORWAY

GERMANY

ITALY

THE NETHERLANDS

SPAIN

ICELAND

UNITED KINGDOM

IRELAND

BELGIUM

FRANCE

SWITZERLAND

PORTUGAL

EUROPE

THE 60 YEARS BETWEEN 1964 AND 2024 IN EUROPE CAN ALMOST BE EVENLY SPLIT BETWEEN THE ERAS OF "COLD WAR" AND "POST-COLD WAR."

FROM THE ERECTION of the Berlin Wall in 1961 to its dismantling in November 1989, the eastern part of Europe was behind the "Iron Curtain." It was the Soviet Union and its communist satellites — and their nuclear arsenal — competing with the West, which included a split Germany, post-World War II economies in France and Italy, and Spain and Portugal going through revolutions. Hard to realize in 2024, but those three decades were filled with stifling threats, spying, troop movements, subterfuge and political meddling.

Western Europe's strategy centered on military strength, capitalism and trade. It began with the North Atlantic Treaty Organization (NATO), formed in 1949.

That alliance was followed by creation of the European Common Market in 1957, comprising West Germany, France, Belgium, Italy, the Netherlands and Luxembourg. It expanded in 1973 with the United Kingdom, Ireland and Denmark. Greece joined in 1981, followed by Spain and Portugal in 1986.

Then the wall fell. Soviet satellites like Romania, Bulgaria, Czechoslovakia (which would divide in 1993), Poland and Hungary went off on their own, and the Soviet Union itself dissolved in December 1991.

The last 30 years have seen an unprecedented consolidation. The European Common Market became the European Union in 1993. Austria, Finland and Sweden joined in 1995. A new currency, the Euro, replaced the franc, deutschmark, lira and other national currencies in 1999.

In 2004 the EU attracted 10 new members, including Poland, Lithuania, the Czech Republic and Slovenia. Bulgaria and Romania followed in 2007, Croatia in 2013.

Frictions and rivalries still exist. Invasions and wars still occur. But there is hope that the interdependence among the European countries will limit the destruction and, instead, induce peaceful co-existence.

United Kingdom
Andy Stevenson

Place of Birth:
Glasgow, Scotland, United Kingdom

Current Residence:
London, England, United Kingdom

UK

Tell me about your family:
My father was a road builder, my mother an office worker and I am the youngest of their six children. I married in 1988 and have two daughters and three grandchildren.

What is the most important lesson that your family taught you?
My father once said that all a parent could hope for was that his children did better in life than them. When he died, I certainly believe he would've felt he fulfilled that. I'm hoping for the same with my brood.

What's your biggest fear?
Dying alone.

What is your greatest pride?
That I was never "found out" for being the talentless hack I am!

What was the favorite time of your life?
Every time I got on an airplane to go somewhere new. Even today I find it hard to accept that I found a job that *paid* me to travel the world and witness events.

What is the best decision you made?
In 1984, when I got a call offering me a two-week assignment in a country called Lebanon, I took 0.2 seconds to say yes! (Even though I had scarcely an idea where Lebanon was or what exactly was going on there.) I wasn't hired for my brains!

What is the best thing about where you live?
Connections. Both travel and personal.

How has life changed in your country since you were a child?
I remember growing up watching a TV show called *Space 1999*. We were all supposed to be living on the moon by now. I guess the serious answer would be the slow death of manufacturing in the United Kingdom during my lifetime. I struggle to think of something made in Britain today. The country seems to exist on financial services and tourism.

What has been the most important event in your country in your lifetime?
Two elections. The election of Margaret Thatcher in 1979, which led directly to the end of many industries in the name of modernization, and Tony Blair in 1997, a time of incredible optimism but which culminated in the United Kingdom's participation in the Iraq war.

How has your view of work changed over time?
In so many ways and none of them good. I entered journalism in 1984 and have witnessed the descent and almost total disappearance of quality journalism to be replaced by a horrible ethic of the need to be first, rather than accurate. The 24-hour news channels and their unquenchable need for "breaking news" leads to stories being aired and published with almost no fact-checking or care for accuracy at all.

Do you have a hidden talent?

No, unless you count juggling badly.

What advice do you have for the next generation?

The advice I always gave to interns and the younger crowd just setting out on their paths was the importance of friendships. I am happy to admit that I was taken on many assignments for my company rather than my talents. The ability to make and maintain friendships will get you through even the darkest of days.

BIG BEN, PALACE OF WESTMINSTER
LONDON, ENGLAND, UNITED KINGDOM
DAVID DIBERT/UNSPLASH

United Kingdom

Lucien De-Laloi

Place of Birth:
Portsmouth, England, United Kingdom

Current Residence:
Southampton, England, United Kingdom

What is the best thing about where you live?
Being by the water and living in the city center.

How has life changed in your country since you were a child?
My country has become more integrated and continues being influenced by the U.S.A.

What has been the most important event in your country in your lifetime?
The death of our former monarch, Her Royal Highness, Queen Elizabeth II, on Sept. 8, 2022.

How has your view of work changed over time?
My working life has influenced my living life. I have had some great well-paid jobs, but they have never continued for long enough. However, the older I'm getting, I'm more grateful for work and especially if it's what I like doing. I am always committed and do as my employer asks, with a little bit more to give that added sparkle.

Tell me about your family:
I have been with my current partner, Melanie, for 26 years. We met through a show I was performing in and we hit it off immediately. We don't have children, purely because we were both career people and didn't think it important. However, we do often look back and think maybe we should. I have four siblings, three of them have families with children. They are all graduates and are living good lives.

What is the most important lesson your family taught you?
My family had great values but along the way my parents had a lot of bad luck happen to them, being ripped off big-time financially. This affected us throughout our lives because of not getting some things that others had. Like having to rent a home, when we previously owned our own outright.

All these things changed our way of looking at life, which I personally never had a grudge about. Even when growing up, I loved my parents and knew how hard it was for them to raise a family. This gave me the realization that family is strength, especially when working together to get things done.

I feel there is a resilience instilled within each one of us children to be tough and not let life get you down. We feel the challenges sometimes.

What is your biggest fear?
My biggest fear is to lose my life through the action of another. I want to live to a good age like my father and grandfathers. Unfortunately, my mother and grandmother died too soon.

What is your greatest pride?
The greatest pride I have is to perform as a jazz vocalist. I've performed internationally and with some great headline acts, too. Unfortunately, I haven't made it big — yet! — but I'm certainly accomplished enough to do so. I'm obsessed with performing in front of audiences, especially appreciative ones.

What was the favorite time of your life?
Looking back, I loved the time I spent with my grandmother. She lived in a place called

THE QUEEN MARY 2 AT THE CRUISE TERMINAL IN

SOUTHAMPTON, ENGLAND, UNITED KINGDOM

PHOTO BY THE AUTHOR

Brockenhurst in the New Forest. I would spend my summer holidays along with my younger brother there. Every day was an adventure. We could be playing in the woods, climbing trees, jumping across rivers, watching deer or badgers or even on the hunt for wild honey.

Then going to Lymington, where my grandmother had a shop on the town quay. From there we would see friends, go crabbing, swim at the local open-air salt-water baths and keep active on our bicycles until it was time to go back to Brockenhurst, which was a five-mile ride each way.

Do you have a hidden talent?

I have great communication skills at all levels of life and I have also inherited abilities to draw, paint, write, sing, and play music. I feel all these communicative talents are very important in the world we live in.

What is the best decision you made?

I feel the best decision I have made to date was to commit myself to Melanie 26 years ago. This is the longest relationship she or I have ever had, and we have had so many horrific things happen to each of us, we are so glad we've been there for each other. May it continue to be strong and resilient.

What advice do you have for the next generation?

Learn as much as you can, be aware of what's happening around you, and be prepared to assist others as you are willing to receive assistance. If you are close to finishing something, see it through, don't back out.

Be honest with yourself and others. You'll never have a restless night knowing you've lied. Keep physically active throughout your life. Enjoy every single day you are alive.

Nothing is guaranteed and we don't know how long we're here for.

United Kingdom

Mark Lock

Place of Birth:
Peterborough, Cambridgeshire, United Kingdom

Current Residence:
Still Peterborough, so answers are based on the United Kingdom, but I have been working on a contract in Dubai for the last 12 months.

What is the best thing about where you live?

Friends and family, Cathedral City, great pubs and close to the East Coast seaside for short breaks, even days out.

How has life changed in your country since you were a child?

Beyond recognition to a degree. All the area around where I lived and played as a child in the fields and on the rivers, down in the local brick-making yards, is now housing estates and shops and supermarkets. That said, all the old 1960s houses are still there and I actually moved back to the estate where I was born and bought one, a bungalow, and renovated it. One of my school friends lived in it; I bought it off her mum, who went into a care home.

Technology has changed so much. The old red telephone boxes are gone. I also remember when I started my own engineering business in 1985 and got a fax machine. This started the rapid change to speed of work, no longer waiting for inquiries and documents in the mail.

What has been the most important event in your country in your lifetime?

That is a difficult one to answer, important as to for the good, bad, or indifferent. For the bad certainly Covid and the insurmountable disruption to our lives, but I personally feel it actually helped us for the good to refocus on our lives as to what is important and what we could actually live without and cut as household expenditures. For the good, certainly laws on equality for us all.

How has your view of work changed over time?

I have worked more or less nonstop since the age of 12 as a paper boy through to having my own business and then back into employment. I missed part of my children (two boys) growing up due to my business and as a workaholic. I treated my work as priority and that everything was urgent to do. I have since realized that not everything is urgent, albeit people treat it as such. A good, equal percentage of work/life balance is now important, to the point where I would accept less income and cut back on luxuries to enjoy leisure time more.

Tell me about your family:

My mother and father divorced when I was 7 and I lived with my mother and sister. My Uncle John, a clerk to the justices and a man of great character, became a father figure for me. I only had one true uncle and aunty as my mum's brother married my dad's sister. My father died of a heart attack aged 42; I went to his funeral, contrary to my mother's wishes. I sneaked out of school.

Both my granddads worked in the local brick-making yards and they and my nans died when I was in my teens. My uncle and aunty died shortly after one another three years ago. That hit me hard, as they were my adopted mother and father after I fell out with my mother and sister in 2000.

I have two sons from a previous marriage: Liam, 30, and Macaulay, 25. They both live in

London. Liam is a creative director and Macaulay is a dancer, choreographer and videographer. I have been married now for 14 years to Kimmy. We have been together for 20 years. She has a son with three children and two daughters.

What is the most important lesson that your family taught you?

Work hard and play hard, love everyone no matter what their stature in life, and watch the pennies as the pounds will then look after themselves.

What's your biggest fear?

Not being able to sustain an income, as I have no great fall-back position nor huge pension potential and I still want to work and travel with Kimmy. My age in the United Kingdom is seen as a disadvantage, but in Dubai it's an advantage to have experience, knowledge and a "Been There, Done It" T-shirt.

What is your greatest pride?

Starting my business, Midas Technologies, with £100 in the bank and keeping it going for 28 years, employing great people and leaving some great architectural and sculptural legacies.

What was the favorite time of your life?

From 18 to 30. I started technical college, met new friends, started to travel for holidays, raced single-seater racing cars, made parachute jumps, and went to discos and nightclubs.

What is the best decision you made?

Meeting and then marrying Kimmy in 2008. (Although when we bought the 1960s bungalow

to renovate, we picked a fixed mortgage at 2.5 percent for the whole term, which was the best financial decision ever!)

Do you have a hidden talent?

Making people laugh. I'm a joker and prankster.

What advice do you have for the next generation?

Get a good balance between work and leisure time, don't chase the money, and cut your cloth accordingly to the work/life balance you desire. Give freely of hellos, chat, love and kindness, and make friends wherever you go.

PETERBOROUGH CATHEDRAL
PETERBOROUGH, CAMBRIDGESHIRE, UNITED KINGDOM
NICK FEWINGS/UNSPLASH

United Kingdom

Kurt Warren

Place of Birth:
Cwmbran, South Wales, United Kingdom

Current Residence:
Ringwould, England, United Kingdom

What is the best thing about where you live?
The countryside.

How has life changed in your country since you were a child?
We have become more multi-cultural.

What has been the most important event in your country in your lifetime?
I think the worst for our economy was definitely BREXIT. For sadness, it was when our beloved Queen passed away. For pride, the Falklands.

How has your view of work changed over time?
Work to live. When I was young, I lived for work and chased the corporate ladder.

Tell me about your family:
Typical Mum, Dad and five kids. Dad worked, Mum looked after the house and kids. From seven we are now four mums; a youngest sister and middle brother have passed away.

What is the most important lesson that your family taught you?
Manners and respect.

What's your biggest fear?
Not taking full advantage of life.

What is your greatest pride?
My family.

What was the favorite time of your life?
Childhood.

What is the best decision you made?
Joining the Army.

Do you have a hidden talent?
I love woodworking and teaching.

What advice do you have for the next generation?
You have one life. It's not a rehearsal. Live your dreams. Don't sit on the chair dreaming your life. One Life: Live It. So what if you fail at one thing? The next you could be the best in the world. Just get up and try. Travel, see the world, embrace different cultures, say "Please" and "Thank you," do one thing every day that makes you smile and laugh. Don't waste your life. You're a long time dead!

Iceland

Gunnar Holmsteinn Arsaelsson

Place of Birth:
Akranes, Iceland

Current Residence:
Garðabaer, Iceland

What is the best thing about where you live?
Close to work, service, and a great swimming pool! (The Atlantic Ocean!)

How has life changed in your country since you were a child?
In many ways, but fundamentally Iceland has opened up to the world and gone from a very homogenic country with nearly only Icelanders living here to a country with almost 20 percent of the inhabitants as immigrants.

What has been the most important event in your country in your lifetime?
Iceland's European Economic Area agreement with the European Union in 1994.

How has your view of work changed over time?
It is as equally important as it was in the old days.

Tell me about your family:
I'm married, with three kids from wife No. 2, two with the first one.

What is the most important lesson that your family taught you?
The value of happiness.

What's your biggest fear?
More war and right-wing extremism (fascism).

What is your greatest pride?
Doing well at work and with my family.

What was the favorite time of your life?
It is really just these days.

What is the best decision you made?
Becoming a teacher.

Do you have a hidden talent?
I play drums.

What advice do you have for the next generation?
Use your head!

Ireland

Colm Rogers

Place of Birth:
Dublin, Ireland

Current Residence:
Gort, County Galway, in the west of Ireland

What is the best thing about where you live?

I live in a small town called Gort, with a population of about 2,500 people, located about 45 minutes from both Galway and Limerick cities. My town has everything I need: a few supermarkets, a couple of decent pubs, restaurants, a bank, post office, a police station and a church.

It's quite unusual in that about one-quarter of the population is Brazilian. They have been here for about 15 to 20 years and are now part of our community. In recent times we have also welcomed friends from Ukraine, who had to flee war at home.

So, I'm quite happy to say we welcome all into our community and we try to help them if we can and they in turn contribute to our society by getting jobs, sending their kids to our schools, and playing sports. They appreciate where they are now.

We recently celebrated St Patrick's Day and it was very noticeable to see the amount of non-Irish people in our town out on the street, watching the annual parade and wearing green, and, most likely, their kids were in the parade.

Locally I play golf at the nearby golf club, which is really good.

We also have a unique landscape near us called The Burren. This is a 360-square-kilometer area of natural beauty and a UNESCO GeoPark. It is noted for its limestone rock surface, carved smooth by glaciers some 340 million years ago. It is also home to the most incredible flora and fauna — some of it arctic and some Mediterranean in origin — living side by side.

The West Coast of Ireland is spectacular for its large seas, jagged coastline and clean seawater and is a very popular destination for tourists. Our native language, Irish or Gaelic, is still spoken by many in this region.

People are generally very friendly and welcoming and are happy to chat and say hello.

How has life changed in your country since you were a child?

Unfortunately, probably for the worse. We have far too many negative influences affecting us and how we live. This ranges from drug abuse, the misuse and bad impact of social media and the internet, and the knock-on effect of war both in Ukraine and Palestine, as well as the Middle East in general. And, of course, climate change.

Our roads are busier, people are driving faster. A lot of people are addicted to their mobile phones, which I think is a very negative thing. People are living lives much faster than they used to. We have lost some respect for our countryside by way of litter being thrown around and some of our rivers and beaches not being cared for as they should.

And, of course, our children have so much bad stuff being bombarded on them each day. On the plus side, sport is a great tonic and thankfully Ireland is host to some of the best sports in the world from rugby to Gaelic games (football and hurling), soccer, golf and lots more.

We are passionate about our sports and that counterbalances some of the bad aspects of modern-day living.

Our native language is undergoing somewhat of a revival and there may be the prospect of a United Ireland at some point in the future.

What has been the most important event in your country in your lifetime?

I would think it would probably have been "the Troubles" in the North, which began in 1969 and ended in 1998. Don't forget the North of Ireland was more or less an apartheid society where Nationalists or Catholics were discriminated against in terms of housing, jobs and the right to vote.

The 1969–70 civil rights movement tried to make change by marching. Things took a bad turn when 13 unarmed civilians were shot dead by the British army. You then had more than 30 years of civil and political conflict, resulting in nearly 3,000 people being killed.

This was not sustainable and eventually — thanks to the intervention of many people in high office — an agreement was reached on Good Friday 1998 recognizing the rights of all citizens, no matter what their religion or political persuasion might be.

Fast-forward to the present day and we have a government in the North headed up by Sinn Féin, a predominantly nationalist party and most likely soon to be in power here in the South.

That, by any stretch, is a huge turnaround. This will hopefully result in a New Ireland for all: Irish, British, Nationalist, Unionist, non-Irish, non-white, gay, trans, you name it; all will be included and respected, as long as they respect their country.

How has your view of work changed over time?

Yes, particularly since Covid, the idea of working silly hours and not having a balance of rest, leisure and work is discouraged. I have a better perspective of how I should live now.

Tell me about your family:

My parents have passed away, both in 1998. I have three brothers and one sister. All live in Ireland. I am divorced and have two beautiful daughters, Kate, 29, and Lisa, 27. Kate lives in Dublin and Lisa is in Vancouver. I have had a great partner for the past 11 years, Sinéad, and she lives about 40 minutes from me. We get on very well and see each other regularly. By mutual agreement we don't live together and will not marry. It works very well as it is.

What is the most important lesson that your family taught you?

This is a hard one! Probably that there is more to life than marriage! Five siblings, five separations and/or divorces! Speaks for itself!

What's your biggest fear?

Death and not knowing what's on the other side.

What is your greatest pride?

My daughters.

What was the favorite time of your life?

I'd say probably now. I still have reasonable health so I'm active.

What is the best decision you made?

Moving to the west of Ireland.

Do you have a hidden talent?

Yes, I can speak Op. This is where you put in op before every vowel sound.

What advice do you have for the next generation?

Take care of each other and the planet and do what you can to avoid conflict.

COUNTY GALWAY, IRELAND

FRANS VAN HEERDEN/PEXELS

VIEW FROM THE RING OF KERRY LOOKOUT, COUNTY KERRY, IRELAND
NILS NEDEL/UNSPLASH

Ireland

Eunan Smyth

Place of Birth:
Limerick, Ireland

Current Residence:
Blackrock, County Louth, Ireland

What's the best thing about where you live?
The sea, the fresh air, the natural beauty.

What is your biggest fear?
From purely a personal view, becoming ill and dependent on others.

How has life changed in your country since you were a child?
The economy improving brought good and bad, a better way of life for most but the ability to afford the more harmful things in life also, like drugs.

What is your greatest pride?
Oh, there's so many things that I'm proud of, each one as important as the next in their own right.

What has been the most important event in your country in your lifetime?
The Good Friday Peace Agreement (between the British and Irish governments) in 1998 that brought peace to this little island.

What was the favorite time of your life?
The last 10 to 12 years, watching my children and grandchildren progress.

How has your view of work changed over time?
If you don't enjoy it, do something else. If you enjoy your job, you'll never do a hard day's work.

What is the best decision you made?
Again, so many decisions, each one as good as the next in its own context.

Tell me about your family:
Two daughters, one son, all happy, healthy and living close by.

Do you have a hidden talent?
The ability to not judge others on first impressions.

What is the most important lesson that your family taught you?
Life hasn't always been plain sailing, but if a family sticks together, they can overcome any situation.

What advice do you have for the next generation?
Don't judge others on first impressions; the book might be much better than the cover shows!

Norway

Eric Krogsgaard Ericsson

Place of Birth:
Stockholm, Sweden

Current Residence:
Oslo, Norway

What is the best thing about where you live?

My husband, my social life with good friends, my work and colleagues. Oslo has never been a favorite city, even though it's got a lot of fine qualities. However, the older I get the less important I find the backdrop. I enjoy my life in this city to the full through family and friends and work I love.

How has life changed in your country since you were a child?

I grew up in Sweden and moved to Norway at the age of 40. During that time, Sweden has changed into a more open and multi-cultural society.

During the last 30 years there has been a great change, considering the definition of Sweden as a hetero-normative, white, Christian patriarchy into a multi-cultural, multi-religious, queer society embracing a multitude of family settings and gender diversity. The nuclear family is more or less invalidated as the only way to live a good and happy life. Religious institutions have both lost and gained ground. Most people still consider themselves spiritual, but the thought of belonging to a religious society is less important to some but even more important to some.

Swedish social welfare has been on constant attack from right-wing politicians but is still close to the heart of the Swedes. However, there has been a lot of privatization regarding, for instance, schools and health care due to the conservative wave of the 1980s, so there is in a way a greater class difference than when I was a kid.

Migration through wars and political oppression in other countries has made a larger impact on society than before. Swedes like to look at themselves as an open and tolerant society but, unfortunately, this has nourished right-wing extremism.

All these quite drastic and fast changes have turned the political and religious landscape from the consensus based on social-democratic values in the 1970s into the political and religious polarization of present day.

In my view, Sweden is in the midst of a major redefinition and a bit confused, but I trust its basic humanistic values to be strong enough to move it in a direction that still appreciates the freedom of every individual.

I cannot relate to Norway as a child, since I moved here at the age of 40.

What has been the most important event in your country in your lifetime?

Politically, I must say the murder of Prime Minister Olof Palme in 1986. In a way, Sweden lost its innocence and overnight discovered it was no longer immune to terrorism.

In Norway, the July 22, 2011 shootings at Utøya Island and bombing of the government building, both executed by a right-wing extremist, had the same effect. Both events, however, have put focus on the necessity to defend democracy and humanism every day.

Personally, the gay rights movement has, in time, made my life as a gay man normalized, even though the fight is far from over. There are still homophobic elements threatening the gay society — due to the political or religious bigotry

— and, as late as in July 2022, two men were shot dead outside a gay café in Oslo.

How has your view of work changed over time?

I have always thought working was fun but have not always been content at work. I have worked as an actor, hotel receptionist, streetcar conductor — you name it. Work has been changeable but my social life is the No. 1 important thing. Now, as I have turned 60, I'm happy to say I have found the ultimate job, where I will stay as long as I am able. This is the first time I want to be faithful to my workplace.

Tell me about your family:

Married to my husband, Ole, since 2004. In a relationship since 2002. Due to legislation, gay marriages were not allowed until 2009, but you could, however, register partnership. Ole, born in 1965, works as an arts teacher at a primary school in a suburb of Oslo but was born in a rural valley in mid-southern Norway.

The family I grew up with consists of my parents and two brothers. I have two nephews.

My father, born in 1937 in Stockholm, Sweden, worked as a librarian the last 10 years of his working life, having had a multitude of different jobs beforehand. My mother, born in 1939 in Copenhagen, Denmark, worked as a biomedical analyst and stayed true to the profession all through her professional life.

What is the most important lesson that your family taught you?

Indirectly I learned independence. For several reasons, my parents were not always there for me, so at an early age, I had to learn to care for myself. At the age of 10, I with no problem traveled by bus or train anywhere in Sweden on my own, and could find my way anywhere I liked just using a map.

Ever since I moved away from home at the age of 20, I have been economically independent, not relying on — or receiving, for that matter — money from my parents. Sometimes it's a painful lesson to learn but also a quite useful one.

What's your biggest fear?

Of course, losing Ole and all the different sicknesses that might impair my life, but more directly, I fear the totalitarian turn the world has taken after a long period of humanistic progress. It's disturbing to follow the developments in Eastern Europe, Russia, China and even the United States and the dismantling of humanistic values.

As a Scandinavian, I feel like I'm living in a peaceful bubble of personal freedom, but I cannot take for granted that the anti-humanistic movement won't have a negative impact on our countries.

What advice do you have for the next generation?

Don't waste your time on a quest for material goods. Remember that only you decide who you are and what will make you happy. Life is change, and as long as you act out of love and respect to yourself and others and Mother Nature, just go with the flow.

What is the best decision you made?

Marrying my husband, Ole, and moving to Norway.

Do you have a hidden talent?

When learning a foreign language, I have a photographic memory, remembering grammatical patterns. I thrive at studying grammar.

What is your greatest pride?

Not letting anyone else but myself define who I am or what I should become.

What was the favorite time of your life?

My formative years were in the 1980s and at that time I felt I was totally present. I wasn't in any way the happiest, but felt the time was mine. Otherwise, I feel I am moving onto a time in my life that will be a new "favorite time of my life" right now.

TURNING TORSO, MALMÖ, SWEDEN
PIPO STOLTZ/PEXELS

Sweden

Peter Schepke

Place of Birth:
Malmö, Sweden

Current Residence:
Vellinge, Sweden

What is the best thing about where you live?
Unconditional love to the closest ones.

What is the most important lesson that your family taught you?
Sweden is a very well-organized country with a low level of corruption and a good standard of living. There are not too many people here and so there is a lot of well-preserved nature.

What's your biggest fear?
That something bad would happen to my daughter.

How has life changed in your country since you were a child?
There has been huge immigration for the last 40 years. Integration has not worked well and, as a result, we have much more criminality today.

What is your greatest pride?
My daughter and the good relationship we have.

What was the favorite time of your life?
Probably age 6–10. I spent a lot of time with my grandparents, on my mother's side. I was very close to them.

What has been the most important event in your country in your lifetime?
I would say the changes because of the immigration. If I should say a single event, I would say joining the European Union and NATO.

What is the best decision you made?
To make a new start at around 40. I applied to 4.5 years of university studies to become an upper secondary (high school) teacher.

Do you have a hidden talent?
I am a handy guy, but I do not try to hide that.

How has your view of work changed over time?
Not much. I was raised Lutheran and cherish hard work.

What advice do you have for the next generation?
Changes in climate are natural, the world will not go under. Do not let doomsday people influence your life.

Tell me about your family:
I am divorced with a daughter, 23.

Finland

Ismo Mursu

Place of Birth:
Posio, Lapland, Finland

Current Residence:
Rovaniemi, Lapland, Finland

What is the best thing about where you live?

The best things are clean nature and the changing seasons. Rovaniemi is the biggest city in Europe by area (8,017 square kilometers), but the city center is relatively small.

So, anywhere you live in Rovaniemi, nature is very near. You can drink water from springs and rivers when hiking in the wilderness.

In Lapland, we have more than four seasons; there are eight of them. Between the main seasons are seasons that are a combination of two main seasons. For example, between winter and spring, we have spring-winter in April, when we have daylight for 17–18 hours, but the next day can be like real winter. Between summer and autumn, there is autumnal summer; today can be 20 degrees Celsius, and tomorrow it can snow.

How has life changed in your country since you were a child?

A lot. When I was a child in the early 1970s, most people lived in the countryside, and many worked in agriculture and forestry.

In the 1980s, more people started to move from the countryside to towns or cities, mainly to southern Finland and near our capital, Helsinki.

Nowadays, 20 percent of the Finnish population lives around Helsinki. The Lapland population has decreased from 210,000 to 175,000 in the last 20 years.

Most people in Lapland work in the service and tourism sectors. When I was a child, there was almost no tourism; now, hundreds of thousands of tourists visit Lapland yearly.

Also, in my childhood, Finland was a non-aligned country, but now we are a member of NATO.

What has been the most important event in your country in your lifetime?

In 1975, in late July and early August, Finland arranged the first conference of the OSCE — Organization for Security and Cooperation — in Europe. It was attended by every head of state in every OSCE member country.

The first world athletics championship was held in Helsinki in 1983.

On January 1, 1995, Finland joined the European Union. From an individual's perspective, freedom of movement within the Schengen area and the common currency, the euro, have been the most significant points of joining the EU.

How has your view of work changed over time?

I am a retired army officer. There, I was always sure I'd keep my job until retirement, and that's it. Surprisingly, I currently have a part-time job as a professional tour guide in the tourism industry at Apukka Resort Rovaniemi. I can use all my skills to take guests snowmobiling in snowy nature or ice fishing on a frozen lake.

Tell me about your family:

My mother is still living; she is 20 years older than me, but my father passed away a couple of years ago. I also have a sister who is four years younger than me. I'm divorced; my family consists of five children and five grandchildren.

What is the most important lesson that your family taught you?

A good person gives even from a little; an evil person not even if they have a lot to share.

What's your biggest fear?

Nowadays, the world has become so crazy and cruel that I fear a couple of world leaders losing the rest of their minds. Even though Lapland is a very safe place to live, I am concerned about the youngest kids every time they visit the cities of southern Finland.

What is your greatest pride?

For the last 20 years of my life, I have been able to spend much of my time with my children. We have shared hobbies together, such as athletics, karting, and fishing.

What was the favorite time of your life?

For sure, childhood in the countryside of Posio in the late 1970s.

What is the best decision you made?

My best decision is that I have tried my best to spend as much time as possible with my youngest children and do things together that we all like.

Do you have a hidden talent?

No one has ever beaten me in a game of Trivial Pursuit! However, I haven't played it in at least 10 years.

What advice do you have for the next generation?

Youngsters — treat others as you want to be treated! Believe in yourselves and you can change the world for the better.

Lithuania

Kestutis Lukoskinas

Place of Birth:
Vilnius, Lithuania

Current Residence:
Vilnius, Lithuania

What is the best thing about where you live?

It's a green, uncrowded city and clean country with as yet unspoiled nature. The place where you can plainly experience all four seasons of the year. It is also a social turmoil-free area.

How has life changed in your country since you were a child?

Remarkably. I was born and lived until young adulthood in a lie-filled, repressive Soviet Union. After the "Singing Revolution" (events leading up to the end of Soviet rule in the Baltic nations), now I live in a free, independent, democratic Western country, a member of the European Union and NATO.

The majority of citizens are happy but, of course, there is a small (disappearing) part of society that misses the Soviet times when the state "took care" of everything and everyone. Younger generations don't understand (and don't care) about the Soviet past. They normally worry about the present day and trying to build a better future.

What has been the most important event in your country in your lifetime?

The proclamation and regaining of independence in 1990. The 1990s were tough (the "Wild East") but in the years since Lithuania (and other Baltic states, Latvia and Estonia) has achieved more than other Western countries in 100 years. Lithuania is prospering.

How has your view of work changed over time?

For almost half of my life I have done what I like the most (organizing and handling travel for visitors).

Tell me about your family:

My father was an opera singer and conductor. He was very talented but an alcoholic. It consumed him and he passed away. My mother was an economist and a purchasing manager. She couldn't stand my father's problems with alcohol and divorced him. I have two brothers — older and younger, both more or less happily married with kids. I have never been married and am living with my female partner. I don't have kids.

What is the most important lesson that your family taught you?

I was raised to be patient and forgiving but to stand up for justice.

What's your biggest fear?

That the Western world will betray Ukraine and later World War III will break out.

What is your greatest pride?

Lithuania — my country, its history, its ups and downs.

What was the favorite time of your life?

All stages of life were interesting. Some tough, some comfortable. Still is that way.

What is the best decision you made?

To go to study philosophy to broaden my views and sensitivity.

Do you have a hidden talent?

Drawing.

What advice do you have for the next generation?

Don't give in to laziness, selfishness, and vanity. Break out of the rat race and practice living slower. Stand up for justice.

UŽUPIS DISTRICT, VILNIUS, LITHUANIA
GEDIMINAS MEDZLAUSIS/ISTOCKPHOTO

Russia

Vladimir Yurievich Lebedev

Place of Birth:
Town of Tyoplaya Gora,
Perm Region (Ural Mountains), Russia

Current Residence:
Moscow, Russia

What is the best thing about where you live?

The people. They are not perfect, but they are close and dear to me.

How has life changed in your country since you were a child?

Life has changed very significantly. I was raised during a time when communist ideology dominated. Now our country has capitalism — market relations and the power of money. There is more freedom now, but also more moral decay and hunger for gain, whereas, I'm sad to say, love and good relations between people are declining.

What has been the most important event in your country in your lifetime?

The most important event in my own life was my coming to know God and being baptized. The most important event in my country, in my opinion, was the transition from socialism to capitalism, and the government's rejection of communist ideology.

How has your view of work changed over time?

For a long time, work was just a difficult but obligatory requirement, just to earn money to support my family. I was in business, thought about money a lot, and really had a dependent relationship to money. About 15 years ago I left the world of business and began serving in the Russian Orthodox Church. Initially, I was a deacon, and then became a priest. I found a calling that brings me joy and inspires me — serving God and people. My income went down,

but there is enough to go around, thank God! I believe I have found my place in life.

Tell me about your family:

My wife, Natalya, and I have been married for 36 years. She is a director at a puppet theater in Moscow. We have three grown children and four grandchildren. Each night at 9 p.m. we get together for a family prayer with the help of Zoom, even though some members of our family are in different countries and cities. We pray about simple things — health, prosperity — and to ask God to help each of us find our place in this world. It seems to me that love does exist in our family.

What is the most important lesson that your family taught you?

Once, I had to move to a different part of Russia for my work. It was a long and painful separation from my family, and it was difficult for me.

During that time away, I made an important discovery — it turns out that family has an essential meaning in my life. I really need the support of people close to me. It was a very important lesson! Now I am very cautious about any long trips or separations, and I value the time we spend together.

What's your biggest fear?

Most of all, I am afraid of sin. Sin — meaning evil thoughts, desires, words, and actions, which can often wound the heart. I fight against sin with all the means at my disposal. And sin also damages my relationship with God, which is so important to me.

What is your greatest pride?

I am gladdened by my children and grandchildren, my relationship with my wife, and also by the fact that, in my working life, I am able to support people.

What was the favorite time of your life?

My favorite time of life is right now!

What is the best decision you made?

To get married and to get baptized.

Do you have a hidden talent?

I would like to learn how to truly love God and other people. I feel that, as of yet, I have not unlocked this talent inside myself. But I do not lose hope that I can learn.

What advice do you have for the next generation?

The most important thing in life is love. I advise people to look for real love (there are a lot of fake kinds in the world), to find that love, to strengthen it, to increase it.

I wish for everyone to be able to attain pure holy love, which is when you love everyone, even your enemies. I am not able to do this myself just yet, but I am actively engaged in learning how to do this.

Poland

Aleksander Kusz

Place of Birth:
Łańcut, Poland

Current Residence:
Łańcut, Poland

What is the best thing about where you live?

I have recently moved to the countryside. It is great because the house is located in a mountainous area. I am living close to my family. I am very grateful to be able to see my grandchildren, my son and his wife and my daughter and her husband so often! I love my neighbors as well. They are very obliging and helpful. We can always count on each other. The area is very picturesque, and great for bicycle trips, which I love.

How has life changed in your country since you were a child?

Life has changed completely. In my childhood, there were no computers or smartphones, life was much more modest. Meat was usually eaten once a week. If I wanted to have my own money, I had to earn it myself. People made money by collecting, drying, and selling herbs, scrap metal, or bottles.

I had two brothers older than me (four and six years older). We always competed in who could collect the most herbs and earn more money from it. It was very exciting and motivating. Even though we lived in a small town, we had three plots of land that needed to be cultivated, as well as breeding nutria, rabbits, and chickens. My parents came from the countryside, and cultivating a plot of land was necessary to feed a large family. Our duties included weeding the plot and taking care of the animals.

My father was an electrician. My mother was a successful seamstress. They were busy working

all day long. I didn't have any toys as a child. I remember once I got a toy car and I broke it. Later, my mother kept saying that because I had broken such a nice car, I never got another toy. But in hindsight, it was good because it shaped creativity.

What has been the most important event in your country in your lifetime?

The first event was when I was in primary school when Russian troops entered Czechoslovakia. There were armored vehicles and cars on top of tanks driving day and night. My parents said there would be a war, but as a child, I didn't really understand it.

At school, they said how cool the USSR and socialism were. The soldiers gave us their uniform buttons, which we could then exchange for something valuable with other colleagues.

The second event was the government's implementation of martial law in 1981. I served in the Navy and was on a ship. At 3 a.m. we were woken up by a combat alarm. We all had to go to our fighting stations. I was in hydroacoustics — I was detecting submarines. I was so worried that I'd be forced to go to the street and shoot Poles, my countrymen. I thought that I would not obey an order if I received one. Fortunately, nothing like that happened.

How has your view of work changed over time?

I was always attracted to trade, which was probably in my genes because my grandfather had a shop before the war and my mother also had a knack for trade. As a young man, I wanted to earn well, but in order to settle down in life, I couldn't count on my parents' help.

I graduated from high school and started working in accounting, which was very boring. After the army, I took a job in a crystal-cutting shop, where I obtained the title of journeyman. In the meantime, I started selling some products on the markets. It turned out that I could earn much more on this trade than at work. Unfortunately, difficult times came and the products stopped selling, and the boss closed the company. Later I opened a grocery store and ran my own business for 15 years. I decided that it is better than working for someone else, although it is sometimes more difficult.

Tell me about your family:

My ex-wife and I raised two wonderful children, a son and a daughter, who are doing very well in life. We have four wonderful grandchildren: three girls and a grandson.

Our marriage was unsuccessful. But, apparently, we brought great values to the children's lives and taught them how to cope with life. After many years spent together and building a house, our children went their separate ways and the house was empty. Fortunately, my daughter and her family live there now.

We started our lives again. My ex-wife has a new husband and I have a wonderful wife and a new home. We all meet at various events, me with my wife and my ex-wife with her husband. I am very happy about the fact that we do not feel any resentment towards each other and we still see each other. I love my children and grandchildren very much and I can't imagine it being any different.

What is the most important lesson that your family taught you?

It doesn't matter how old you are, everyone can be your teacher, even someone younger than you. You can't think that you are the center of the world and your children are stupid. I have learned a lot from my children and I am sure my children have learned a lot from me as well. Caring for each other and listening to what each other has to say is the basis of mutual respect.

What's your biggest fear?

Being disabled and having someone take care of me is my biggest fear. I want to be fit for the rest of my life and die without causing trouble to anyone.

What is your greatest pride?

I am very proud of what my children have achieved. I am proud that they are doing very well in life. My son has a successful company. My daughter runs blogs and publishes cookbooks. She implements new ideas all the time, which is how she and her husband make a living.

I am proud that I have a wonderful, wise, and very hard-working wife and that at such a late age I managed to find the love of my life, which sometimes seems unbelievable to me.

What advice do you have for the next generation?

Never complain. Love, and be loved. Listen to what people have to say. Be patient, helpful, and do good deeds for other people, because good always comes back. Move a lot and do sports. Develop your passions and interests. Have friends and always have a goal in life, because life without a goal makes no sense.

What was the favorite time of your life?

The times of high school were great, when I went to summer camps and played the guitar at various celebrations and bonfires. I also played in a band after parties and weddings. School discos were also unforgettable and this was a wonderful youth. The times of raising children were wonderful when you could watch them grow up and become wiser. I always believe that at any age you can live a full life and enjoy it, as long as your health is good.

That is why it is so important to me that I have such a wonderful wife, children who have loving partners, and amazing grandchildren. This period of life that I have now is also perfect for me.

What is the best decision you made?

While serving in the navy, I sang in a band and was hired to join the navy stage band. However, I gave it up and it was a good decision; otherwise, life would have turned out differently.

Do you have a hidden talent?

I'm constantly discovering what new things I can do. I play the guitar, I sing, and I have a YouTube channel. I like it very much. And apart from that, I still do some work around the house. I can make a bench, build a shelter, a shed. Is it my talent? I don't know.

Slovakia

Pavol Bujňák

Place of Birth:
Košice, Czechoslovakia

Current Residence:
Bidovce, Slovakia

What is the best thing about where you live?
Clean air, peace.
I like country life.

How has life changed in your country since you were a child?
Very much so and to the positive. For example, under socialism until 1989, there was the impossibility of traveling freely, there were guarded borders, there was a prohibition of private business, and government controlled all activities. Some people were persecuted by the state police for their opinions. The money system was set by the state through earnings. It was limited by tables (which controlled and determined the amount of money for individual positions).

What was the most important event in your country during your lifetime?
In November 1989, Czechoslovakia's "Velvet Revolution" ended the communist rule associated with the Soviet Union. We gained freedom and it was the end of totalitarianism. Czechoslovakia was dissolved at the end of 1992, becoming Slovakia and the Czech Republic. Slovakia gained entry into the European Union and the North Atlantic Treaty Organization in 2004.

How has your view of work changed over time?
We can do business freely now.
I have my own company.

Tell me about your family:
I was divorced once, and now I'm happily married. I have two children, my wife also has two. Together we have eight grandchildren.

What is the most important lesson your family taught you?
My parents raised me to be honest and modest.

What is your biggest fear?
The loss of freedom and civil rights and the onset of totalitarianism.

What is your greatest pride?
My second relationship and my wife.

What was the favorite time of your life?
Tramping across the country as a youth and woodcraft. Tramping is a traditional Czechoslovak wandering through nature without rules, but with respect and love for nature. Campfires, guitars, singing, and sleeping under the open sky. Woodcraft is forest life in nature and survival.

What is the best decision you made?
To go live in the countryside.

Do you have a hidden talent?
Yes, musically, I play the guitar.

What advice do you have for the next generation?
Protect your freedoms and the environment.

Czech Republic

Vladimir Valenta

Place of Birth:
Brno, Czechoslovakia

Current Residence:
Brno, Czech Republic

CZECH REPUBLIC

What is the best thing about where you live?

The city of Brno is big enough for me to find everything I need for my life in one place, but at the same time too small to suffer from the ills of big cities. I live in a nice neighborhood close to nature and other interesting places. I am a big Brno patriot.

How has life changed in your country since you were a child?

Fundamentally. During my childhood we were part of the socialist bloc and behind the "Iron Curtain." We are now part of a global European space with unlimited possibilities. The new reality has surpassed all our dreams.

What was the most important event in your country during your lifetime?

The "Gentle Revolution" of November 17, 1989, which ended the period of socialism in our country. This was a major social turning point for all of us.

How has your view of work changed over time?

Before the revolution, we had socialism and people's work commitment was very low. After the revolution came the era of early capitalism and unlimited possibilities, and we worked very hard indeed. Now it's stable and I realize the value of a work/life balance.

Tell me about your family:

I am married and live with my wife in Brno. We have a son. He is 32 years old and lives with his girlfriend in Prague. They don't have children, so we don't have any grandchildren yet.

Of our parents, only my father is alive. He is 86 years old and lives in Brno.

What is the most important lesson your family taught you?

That there is strength in unity and that we all have to help each other.

What is your biggest fear?

From the current development of society, which is moving towards populism and authoritarianism. It manifests itself not only in our country but throughout Europe and the whole world.

What is your greatest pride?

That, despite my advanced age, I manage to keep up with the times.

What was the favorite time of your life?

My youth. That will never come back. :-) But I've enjoyed all the seasons of my life and I wouldn't turn back time.

What is the best decision you made?

That was 36 years ago. I married my wife.

Do you have a hidden talent?

I haven't discovered any such talent yet, but maybe it's just too well hidden :-).

What advice do you have for the next generation?

Always use your own head and don't be manipulated. Embrace critical thinking above all.

VIEW OF THE CATHEDRAL OF ST. PETER AND PAUL FROM SPILBERK CASTLE, BRNO, CZECH REPUBLIC

SANGA PARK/ISTOCKPHOTO

Switzerland

Ivo Haefliger

Place of Birth:
Lucerne, Switzerland

Current Residence:
Zug, Switzerland

What is the best thing about where you live?

I live in a country that offers a very high quality of life, a functioning democracy, stability, beautiful landscapes, cities and towns, and a good location from where to travel abroad.

How has life changed in your country since you were a child?

The new technologies have fundamentally changed the way we interact with family, friends, business partners and government. The high increase of immigrants has made the country more crowded, especially when it comes to transportation and availability of housing.

What has been the most important event in your country in your lifetime?

The fact I live in Switzerland in a direct democracy with regular votes for referendums and initiatives (taking place several times every year) makes every vote a very important event as we participate in decisions and can change how things are.

How has your view of work changed over time?

I see the change mainly in the use of technology, which makes communication much easier and also allows work from anywhere in the world.

Tell me about your family:

I have a very nice family that offers stability, advice and security. I am glad my parents, both over 80 years old, are still very active.

What is the most important lesson that your family taught you?

Be friendly with everyone and get a good education.

What's your biggest fear?

The political situations in many countries around the world and the environment issues that are causing a threat to humankind, animals and the world in general.

What is your greatest pride?

That I have traveled to many places around the world (126 countries through today), making me understand cultural differences and getting a better view of the world.

What was the favorite time of your life?

There is no favorite time in my life, as every time has had its advantages and disadvantages.

What is the best decision you made?

To reduce work after I had turned 50 and start to enjoy life more.

Do you have a hidden talent?

I think I have a talent for painting, which I do not really explore.

What advice do you have for the next generation?

Reduce time in the virtual world and live more in the real world and understand that there are different ways to do and see things.

Austria

Rainer Lefevre

Place of Birth:
Wiener Neudorf, Austria

Current Residence:
Vienna, Austria

What is the best thing about where you live?
My place of residence is in the city and yet in the countryside.

How has life in your country changed since you were a child?
Everything has become more hectic and faster. There is much less freedom and privacy.

What was the most important event in your country during your lifetime?
Austria's accession to the European Union in 1995.

How has your view of work changed over time?
I work in tourism and social media has changed the image that tourists have of Vienna and Austria.

What is the most important lesson your family has taught you?
That you only have one life, and it doesn't last forever.

Tell me about your family:
I am married and have two adult children.

What is your biggest fear?
That my children die before me.

What is your greatest pride?
The development of my children.

What was the favorite time of your life?
My childhood.

What was the best decision you made?
To learn my profession.

Do you have a hidden talent?
I can listen.

What advice do you have for the next generation?
Use all resources carefully and sustainably.

GOLDEN HALL OF THE MUSIKVEREIN WIEN, VIENNA, AUSTRIA

J/UNSPLASH

Slovenia

Marjan Požek

Place of Birth:
Bela Krajina, Yugoslavia

Current Residence:
Koper, Slovenia

What is the best thing about where you live?
The sea, climate, and nature.

How has life changed in your country since you were a child?
Life in our country has changed many times, as we have experienced major political changes. First, we were in Yugoslavia under the leadership of Josip Broz Tito, and then in 1991, Slovenia, the country I live in, became an independent parliamentary republic. Koper, the city where I live, has turned from a small harbor town into a large city with approximately 60,000 inhabitants. It is among the most important ports in Europe. The surrounding fields and pastures have turned into settlements, trade centers and business centers.

What was the most important event in your country in your life?
Certainly it was the call for independence in June 1991, when we separated from Yugoslavia, and the ensuing Ten-Day War that this decision brought about. The second is the adoption of the Euro currency in 2007, where at the beginning items were more expensive but it became easier to trade with neighboring countries, especially with Italy, which we border.

How has your view of work changed over time?
Work has changed mainly in technology and speed of work, although we still have only 24 hours in a day. But because of computers, we can put extra work in (and feel stress). What we did in one week 30 years ago, we can now do in one day, which is an obvious burden for people and the consequences are visible.

Tell me about your family:
We were a simple farming family — father, mother and sister, making a living from agriculture and animal breeding until my sister and I went to university and our own professions.

What is the most important lesson that your family taught you?
Working hard and saving and being diligent doesn't always bring you optimal results. Follow your own path, not others'. Analyze situations and adapt to them.

What's your biggest fear?
I don't have any more fears. I've experienced and survived many things since the war, like cancer. Now I live every day to the fullest and I don't pay attention to the fears that quickly confuse your head and put you in a bad mood.

What is your greatest pride?
My children, that they followed their own path, they are successful and did not cause any problems. They have their lives as they planned it and they do not regret anything.

What was the favorite time of your life?
Of course, the marriage with my long-term wife and the birth of my two children and their successes, in business and personal life.

What is the best decision you made?

Leaving my regular job and going on a business adventure with a friend.

Do you have a hidden talent?

I love to draw and create from parchment paper, from greeting cards to paintings to 3-D realistic buildings.

What advice do you have for the next generation?

Life is beautiful, but at the same time, it can be very short. Don't waste time with nonsense. Take care of your finances and security for the future. Trust yourself and your loved ones, find a partner who will love and support you, and, above all, trust yourself!

Greece

Kosmadakis Spyros

Place of Birth:
Herakleion, Crete, Greece

Current Residence:
Herakleion, Crete, Greece

What is the best thing about where you live?
The sun.

How has life in your country changed since you were a child?
Virtual goods vs. real goods. Communication is better. Home living but with a more driven level.

What was the most important event in your country in your life?
The negative fact that Covid has changed life forever here.

How has your view of work changed over time?
Three days a week are enough for the oldest six-day production.

Tell me about your family:
We are a family of four with two 14-year-old boys.

What is the most important lesson your family taught you?
Love humanity.

What is your biggest fear?
Epidemics, natural disasters.

What is your greatest pride?
My family.

What was your favorite moment in life?
The baptisms of my children.

What's the best decision you've made?
To settle in Crete.

Do you have a hidden talent?
Many.

What advice do you have for the next generation?
Choose real in-person communication, socialize, and read physical books.

Italy

Massimo Mannu Sassari

Place of Birth:
Sardinia, Italy

Current Residence:
Sindia, Nuoro Province, Sardinia, Italy

Tell me about your family:
I have a wife, three children, and eight grandchildren.

What is the best thing about where you live?
Having the sea nearby, since it is possible to go there about seven months a year, with a bright sun.

What is the most important lesson that your family taught you?
The value and importance of the word "family," that is, the union between parents and children in life.

What's your biggest fear?
That something bad will happen to someone in my family.

What is your greatest pride?
My children and grandchildren.

What was the favorite time of your life?
The best time of my life was my 40s. At that age a man achieves his best psycho-physical result in life.

What is the best decision you made?
To get married and have children.

Do you have a hidden talent?
My hidden talent is cooking, as I'm in love with cooking fantastic and delicious dishes, even though I can't totally express this talent of mine.

What advice do you have for the next generation?
My advice is to resume human relationships as the technological tools that exist now are making sure that people don't talk to each other.

How has life changed in your country since you were a child?
It has changed completely because the technology has moved forward and the way of living and communicating is very different.

What has been the most important event in your country in your lifetime?
As a good Italian, there have been many important events but at the same time none, as we easily forget the good and bad things.

How has your view of work changed over time?
The change in work is caused by technology and the way of communicating with people. Before, in my work as a representative, I went to visit them in person always, even my customers who did not even have a landline phone. Now without having to go there personally, you can communicate with them with video calls, messages, emails etc.

Spain

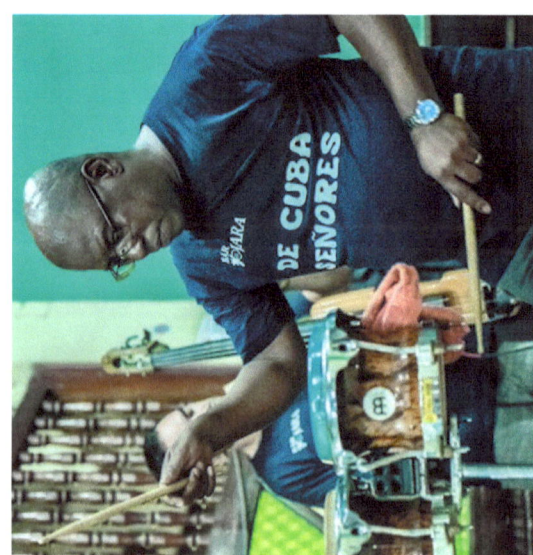

Lazaro Arencibia Ruiz

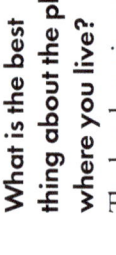

Place of Birth:
Camaguey, Cuba

Current Residence:
Valencia, Spain

What is the best thing about the place where you live?
The beach environment and the multiculturalism.

How has life in your country changed since you were a child?
In Cuba, from 100 to zero. I mean, so much change. From good to bad. There were more possibilities to develop as a happy child and now it is not the case. The prospects for the future are worse.

What has been the most important event in your country during your life?
The protests in the streets of Cuba in July 2021, because it was a social event of political demonstration against the government that has existed since I was born.

How has your view of work changed over time?
For me, it has changed in such a way that after studying music for so many years at university level, I now can do nothing of what I have studied because I am out of my country and my degrees don't have the same value. So I cannot do what I studied.

Tell me about your family:
My family is very big and very united. One person's problem is resolved by everyone. We all support each other.

What is the most important lesson your family taught you?
Respect for other human beings.

What is your biggest fear?
Losing one of my children.

What is your greatest pride?
Being a father.

What was your favorite moment of your life?
The birth of my first child.

What is the best decision you made?
Not to have studied a military career.

Do you have a hidden talent?
Drawing and painting.

What advice do you have for the next generation?
To fight every day for a better world.

Portugal

José Alfredo Ramirão Costa

Place of Birth:
Sao Tomé and Príncipe, Portugal

Current Residence:
Mealhada (near Coimbra), Portugal

What is the best thing about where you live?

Quality of life! (Weather; employment; security; culture; diversity of landscape; gastronomy; social care/health services; inclusion.)

How has life changed in your country since you were a child?

It happened with a very strong change in April 1974 with a political revolution, a transition from a dictatorial regime to a democratic regime. Later, we entered the European Union and the global market. The technological effects changed the labor market and created a lot of opportunities for people — better salaries; an emphasis on human rights (especially women's rights and children's rights); better services (health and social security); and better education at the upper levels.

What has been the most important event in your country in your lifetime?

The transition from a dictatorial regime to a democratic regime, indeed! — the Revolution of April 25, 1974. I remember participating in some "revolutionary" activities at school. Very exciting times.

How has your view of work changed over time?

Well, I was always very curious about culture and human life, social issues and economics in other countries. I was a son of an immigrant family that moved to the United States in the 1980s.

Today, I have a sister who has been there since she was 15 years old.

I'm a school psychologist and I'm always concerned about education and training around the Europe and other countries in the world. For that, I pay special attention to the evolution of work. I do guidance counseling for children at 15 years old.

I've experienced rural life (in my childhood), an urban/university life, and a life in European education and training systems as a school psychologist.

This life matrix gave me a global view about social and technical evolution in the issue of labor. At my work, for example, I finished my university studies in July and I began work in October.

Today, my colleagues have difficulty getting employed in the government system, and a lot of them instead go to others countries in Europe.

Well, that's okay; why not? We are world citizens; we must have this mentality!

I've shared this with my children: Change is a basic condition of life! We must be prepared to change. The labor market and society and culture change, too. It's normal!

Tell me about your family:

My parents were immigrants in Fall River, Massachusetts in the United States for about 20 years. But before, my father was a migrant in Sao Tomé and Príncipe island, off the coast of Africa, near the equator. That is where I was born and lived for two years. Then I came to my grandparents' home in Portugal with my mother and grew up there.

We lived in a little village in the center of the country, a rural and mountain village called Santo Amaro de Tavares. They worked in agriculture. And I helped them when not in school. I studied in the nearest bigger town, Viseu. I did my university studies in Oporto and Coimbra universities, two of the most important universities of Portugal.

I'm married. I have two children, a son and a daughter. They are both engineers and work in the area.

I am a school psychologist and my wife was a kindergarten teacher. She is retired now and I will be in two years.

I lived in Coimbra, Spain until four years ago; now I live 17 kilometers to the north, in Mealhada. It is a very interesting region, known for sparkling wine and toasted piglet. There is an interesting mountain, Serra do Buçaco, and a very old forest planted by Carmelitas monks.

What is the most important lesson that your family taught you?
Be honest, loyal, a good worker, informed, educated, and care about your family.

What's your biggest fear?
Sincerely and suddenly, I don't think about this! Thinking better, it is a war among the world; the extremism and radicalism in political regimes; and the climate changing.

What is your greatest pride?
My children. A nice man and a nice woman!

What was the favorite time of your life?
The present, today — the here and now! My Saturday breakfast at a Portuguese coffee shop — a cup of milk and coffee and a piece of toasted bread with butter, reading a book or a newspaper or writing. Spending time with my family in the rural countryside.

What is the best decision you made?
I stayed in Portugal when my parents and sister emigrated to the United States.

Do you have a hidden talent?
Maybe — but I didn't explore it enough! I like to design and write, or "do nothing" in an esplanada in the center of old cities.

What advice do you have for the next generation?
Have an attitude to find information and pay attention. Analyze and use your critical thinking! Be tolerant! Have an open mind! Be a world citizen!

France

Alex Sysoyev

Place of Birth:
Ukraine

Current Residence:
Northern France

What is the best thing about where you live?
A good climate and friendly people.

How has life changed in your country since you were a child?
Ukraine is well known in the whole world because it is currently engaged in the war against Putin.

What has been the most important event in your country in your lifetime?
Obtaining independence from the Kremlin in Russia in 1991.

How has your view of work changed over time?
Work has to be fun and a way to earn money at the same time.

Tell me about your family:
I am divorced for the second time but trying my best to keep in touch with my two daughters and my son.

What is the most important lesson that your family taught you?
To be generous.

What's your biggest fear?
A nuclear war.

What is your greatest pride?
My son, Pierre.

What was the favorite time of your life?
My childhood when my parents were still young and taking care of me.

What is the best decision you made?
To flee the USSR in 1991.

Do you have a hidden talent?
My intuition, which is normally attributed to women.

What advice do you have for the next generation?
Get rid of communism.

France

Pierre-François Claisse

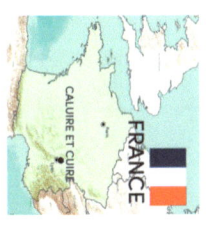

Place of Birth:
Neuvilly, France

Current Residence:
Caluire-et-Cuire, France

What is the best thing about where you live?

Being near a big city with all its advantages, in terms of activities, and being far enough away to enjoy a quiet area.

Tell me about your family:

I have a very nice family, which is the best thing I have ever had in my life. A Canadian wife and three kids — daughter, son, and daughter.

What is the most important lesson that your family taught you?

Work is not all there is in life.

How has life changed in your country since you were a child?

Life has changed a lot since I moved from a small village (about 1,500 people) to a big city (Lyon), which is claimed to be the third biggest in France. There is also the evolution of technology, which everybody my age knows.

What's your biggest fear?

Injuries, death of wife or kids, losing my job.

What is your greatest pride?

It is probably more luck than pride — my family.

What has been the most important event in your country in your lifetime?

Maybe not a very original answer but I would say the Covid pandemic of 2020. It was so unexpected. It had a very big impact on everyone's life.

What was the favorite time of your life?

Sports. I have been running since I was a teenager. I am also an official judge in track and field events.

What is the best decision you made?

To get married to my wife and to have kids.

How has your view of work changed over time?

I have been always very involved in work. Probably still too involved. Nevertheless, over the years it took a smaller place in my life (when I got married, then had kids and now getting closer to retirement). I was always very interested doing new things and having new challenges. I, therefore, switched jobs a few times.

But now as I approach 60, I am considered as being too old for companies to be attractive here in France. I have to say for the time being I have given up looking for other challenges by switching companies, even if I am convinced I can find a good job in a new position in a new company.

Do you have a hidden talent?

I do not know. You'd have to ask my wife, kids and friends.

What advice do you have for the next generation?

Take care of the Earth, yourself and the others. Do not spend too much time on social networks.

Belgium
Dirk Herremans

Place of Birth:
Ninove, Belgium

Current Residence:
Okegem, Belgium

What is the best thing about where you live?

We live 100 meters from the town square, on a small dead-end street, which provides a quiet environment that's still close to the baker, butcher, pub, restaurant, bus stop and train station. The peacefulness and our friend circle make us never want to leave.

How has life changed in your country since you were a child?

The most obvious change is the traffic getting worse, but I think that's the case everywhere. Also, drug use, and the criminality associated with it, has grown significantly. In general, public safety feels diminished.

Politically, the biggest change is that we have lots of different jurisdictions — federal, Flemish, Wallonian, German, and Brussels — hopefully, I haven't forgotten one. Previously there was only one central government. This sometimes leads to problems with decision-making.

What has been the most important event in your country in your lifetime?

For me, the biggest sporting event is the "Tour of Flanders" road cycling race, where hundreds of thousands of cycling fans line the course to cheer the racers on.

How has your view of work changed over time?

Over my career, the production of goods has become highly automated, which is good for workers' health; less heavy lifting is better for the back. My back could've used it.

Tell me about your family:

I was the fifth child born of eight, one of which died at birth and one after a few months. Our parents were self-employed; our father made windows, doors, stairs, garage doors, etc. out of iron and, later, aluminum. Our mother ran a store selling all kinds of housewares, gardening tools and figurines.

I retired a year and a half ago from a cardboard factory. My wife, Christel, and I have two children. Our daughter is a speech therapist and works at a school. She also has two children. Our son has a mental disability and lives at a facility in Dilbeek. He cannot speak but can walk and communicate with gestures.

What is the most important lesson that your family taught you?

Our parents taught us, above all, to be honest and social. You dedicate yourself to the community. And work hard.

What's your biggest fear?

That something will happen to the children or the grandchildren. That they would run into the wrong people.

What is your greatest pride?

Proud of what we achieved through hard work. And proud of everything our daughter does. Working at the school and giving another dozen children extra lessons from home, while also bringing up her own two kids.

What was the favorite time of your life?

For me, it was when I was 16 to 25 years old. I worked in the bakery then and put in a lot of hours, but we had fun and were carefree.

What is the best decision you made?

Building a house 300 meters from our old one.

Do you have a hidden talent?

Betry (my sister) says that I'm good at traveling and organizing trips with the motor home.

What advice do you have for the next generation?

Respect Mother Nature and protect her; you're going to need her. Be honest and friendly with each other. And stay away from drugs and cigarettes.

The Netherlands
Paul Evan Ensley

Place of Birth:
Amsterdam, The Netherlands

Current Residence:
Amsterdam, The Netherlands

What is the best thing about where you live?

After World War II, Queen Wilhelmina of the Netherlands added the motto "Heroic, Determined, Merciful" to the coat of arms of the city of Amsterdam as a tribute to residents' resistance. It says a lot about the intrinsic values of "Amsterdammers" — and I am proud to be part of that mentality.

Nowadays, Amsterdam is a unique melting pot of history and modernity — an open and liberal society with outspoken inhabitants. Almost all nationalities can be found in Amsterdam: the whole world in a compact city, full of different cultures, mixed and intertwined, with the intention of equality and mutual respect.

How has life changed in your country since you were a child?

Coming of age in the 1970s and 1980s, people my age were involved in all sorts of political and social developments. As a real Amsterdammer, I participated in big political demonstrations, houses being squatted, and riots in historic areas against capitalist influences — just like the queen's motto. In the end, we were able to save a lot of our cultural heritage for generations to come.

"We worried about the Cold War, not the planet warming up." That was not a thing to worry about. I believe we were truly socially engaged rebels. We were not ignorant, just totally uninformed about how capitalism can ruin our planet. At present, the shift in mindfulness is not only needed but an intrinsic part of my life and of the younger generations.

What has been the most important event in your country in your lifetime?

Not so much one event, but more a well-needed string of events. Call it a cultural movement.

"May you live in interesting times" — this old Chinese proverb is an ironic curse. If we look back in time to a couple of centuries ago, slavery and exploitation of people overseas are things we cannot be proud of as Dutchies. Yes, we need to apologize for slavery and other wrongdoings. We even need to compensate those whose ancestors suffered and perished. And yes, we need to stop with folkloristic events that offend ethnic groups in our society. And yes, I am a firm believer in change via radical new ideas. But no, not when this leads to bashing and stigmatizing others.

How has your view of work changed over time?

It absolutely has. Over the decades, things that are important to business people have changed. My career started in the mid-1980s as a banker and later on as an advertising/marketing/web guy. It was a material world. We talked in terms of shareholder value, outsourcing, offshoring and increased profitability. Today, we talk about reputation, branding, corporate social responsibility, storytelling, and work/life balance. We went from plain capitalism to human capitalism. And that's really good.

Tell me about your family:

My parents reflect the melting pot that is Amsterdam. My mother has French roots, and my dad was an American country boy. They met when my dad was stationed in the army in Germany in the early 1960s. With a salary in dollars and a great exchange rate to the guilder (our currency before the Euro), he would visit Amsterdam with his army friends. That's how they got together — in the end an unfortunate clash of cultures. Dad missed the states living in the Netherlands, and Mum could not plant her feet in America, missing the Dutch culture, friends and family. If they had met in 2024, things could have turned out quite differently. The Dutch Calvinist attitude 50 years ago and the present liberal and progressive feel of our society could have led to them being successful as partners. Besides, the USA is no longer the promised land it was for Europeans half a century ago; it's a lot more congruent now.

What is the most important lesson that your family taught you?

Not to manifest my life the way my parents did. The melancholy, the cultural gap, the search for happiness — I am grateful for this lesson they gave me, which gave me the right insights into finding a chosen family, being a good dad to my kids, and being a loving partner. Hopefully, my kids will learn from the perceived "mistakes" I've made in guiding them and weave this into their lifestyle. It's the circle of life.

What's your biggest fear?

Fear is not in my vocabulary. Let's call it concerns.

One, climate change. In the Netherlands, we are below sea level and we are known for our engineering skills in water management, including dikes, canals, and windmills. Is our historic city still untouched by water in 100 years?

Two, the European Union is an institution that is not well organized and still practices old-school capitalism. Global developments may hit EU countries hard, and a shift of power is well under way. How will Europe manage to adapt to global developments and circumstances? And what does that mean to our small but still powerful country?

What is your greatest pride?

After realizing that my generation set the premise for the mass exploitation of our fellow people, animals, and earth, I grew determined to be the change I wanted to see in this world. I simply wanted to be aware of the choices I made in life. Buy only the stuff you really need, give your possessions a second life, and stop mindlessly consuming. Think, then act. I also started a plant-based diet four years ago. Those are recommendations I picked up from the conscious lifestyle of youngsters and I am proud to implement it into my lifestyle.

What was the favorite time of your life?

Was or is? It's often said about our generation that we are the first to really look after our parents and our children. Maybe it is true for the (Western-style) capitalist societies, but other communities and societies around the world have been doing this for millennia. What I am trying to say is that the present time is one in which three generations face each other and need to live in harmony whilst existential decisions need to be made. For the generations to come, I am proud to be part of that and have a firm belief humankind will overcome all crises. Live now, and embrace the past as a learning tool.

What is the best decision you made?

Do you flow through life or does life flow through you? A good friend asked this philosophical question during a day of visiting bars downtown. I answered unequivocally: Life flows through me. If you are able to stand still in silence and see what life has to offer to you, choices can be made without compromise.

Do you have a hidden talent?

I was born with creative genes. I am a creator: writing, designing, and all sorts of things. I love to create inspiring environments — either to live in or do business in. This has been a well-hidden talent for a long time. Recently, my partner, Kisa, and I started a marketing and business consultancy company in which we use a method called "Attention, Love, and Encouragement" — creating better businesses by applying the human touch. My partner gave me a well-needed push. You are never too old to expose your hidden talents.

What advice do you have for the next generation?

I haven't been brought up in a world where sustainable choices were made. It wasn't even an issue you would think about. We consumed unconsciously in a world where everything seemed possible because we were simply not aware of the impact of our behavior.

My generation may still have some credibility towards the younger generations Y, Z and so on. So, if I show my ability to improve and change, it's noticeably a good thing. And I have to say, younger generations are so friendly and respectful to me. We were not to our parents; to my generation, they were obsolete, old-fashioned, and understood nothing of modern life.

Younger generations are entitled to say bad things about mine. But they don't; instead, they show respect and empathy. For me, this was fundamental to changing my lifestyle and empowering theirs.

CANALS IN AMSTERDAM, THE NETHERLANDS
AZHAR J / UNSPLASH

Germany

Harald Schaal

Place of Birth:
Stuttgart, Germany

Current Residence:
Munich, Germany

What is the best thing about where you live?

The best is the connection between the Bavarian tradition and a modern and livable city. In addition, the surrounding area, with its lakes and mountains as well as the short distances to neighboring countries such as Italy, Switzerland, Austria or the Czech Republic, offers a variety of interesting leisure and travel opportunities.

How has life changed in your country since you were a child?

Germany has become larger after the unification of East and West Germany. Although they are all Germans, different cultures meet. The cities have grown, also due to immigration from abroad. Tolerance towards foreigners has grown. The technical developments make more demands on people. Life has become "faster." More happens in less time and more is done. Germany has become richer and most of the population has benefited. Egoism has grown.

What has been the most important event in your country in your lifetime?

The reunification of East Germany (GDR) and West Germany (FRG) in 1990.

How has your view of work changed over time?

In the past, people often worked in a company for a lifetime. Today, it is rare to find employees who have been with a company for such a long time. The technical requirements have grown. People do more in less time.

Due to globalization, from which Germany benefits greatly, work in many companies has become more international. There was a long period in which the career was in the foreground. Which is no longer so much the case with the younger generation today.

Tell me about your family:

I grew up in a classic working-class family. My German father was a worker on the German Federal Railway. My Croatian mother was a housewife and did a few side jobs to earn some money. I have two siblings, a brother older by three years and a sister younger by 12 years. My brother studied social sciences and still works in a social home. He has four children. My sister was a policewoman before she moved to the Netherlands to get married and still lives there. She has three children. I studied business administration and have no children. We were born in Stuttgart and grew up there. Since my mother is from Croatia, we had a lot of contact with Croatia and thus grew up bilingual.

What is the most important lesson that your family taught you?

Tolerance and do not forget those who have less.

What's your biggest fear?

To die so suddenly without being able to say goodbye to everyone.

What is your greatest pride?

That I have come from a simple working-class background to become what I am today.

What was the favorite time of your life?

Definitely my entire childhood, which I think has shaped me a lot to this day. Since my mother comes from Croatia, we naturally always had contact there. My parents managed to buy a small house right by the sea on the Adriatic at the end of the 1960s. For us working-class children, that meant six weeks of holiday by the sea every summer, friends from Croatia, getting to know new things, always a little adventure. Visiting my grandmother several times a year, who lived in the simplest peasant conditions in the Croatian countryside, was always an adventure for someone like me from the big city. We enjoyed a very loving upbringing by my mother. It was a wonderful childhood with lots of freedom and opportunities for personal development.

What is the best decision you made?

Moving from Stuttgart to Munich in the late 1990s. It was only here that I developed into who I am today. The city, my professional opportunities and the people here were so different from the somewhat dusty city of Stuttgart.

Do you have a hidden talent?

I'm sure everyone has some hidden talent. Unfortunately, I haven't discovered mine yet.

What advice do you have for the next generation?

Be abroad as often as you can. Learn as many foreign languages as possible. This is the only way to learn tolerance and understanding of other people, countries and cultures.

MARIENPLATZ, MUNICH, GERMANY
DANIEL SESSLER/UNSPLASH

Germany

Joachim Burkhardt

Place of Birth:
Stuttgart, Germany

Current Residence:
Munich, Germany

What is the best thing about where you live?
My home.

How has life changed in your country since you were a child?
Technical progress and the environment.

What has been the most important event in your country in your lifetime?
The birth of our daughter.

How has your view of work changed over time?
Most time it's been positive.

Tell me about your family:
One wife, one girl, it fits together, I think.

What is the most important lesson that your family taught you?
Stay together, and have humor.

What's your biggest fear?
The health first of my daughter, second my wife, and then me.

What is your greatest pride?
Our daughter.

What was the favorite time of your life?
Every day now because in every period in your life, you have so many positive experiences.

What is the best decision you made?
To have a family.

Do you have a hidden talent?
Humor, I think, and to become a golf pro. I forget.

What advice do you have for the next generation?
Have a work/life balance. Keep learning as long as possible and study. Learn what you want, make the job one you like, and be curious.

Germany

Josef Schiessl

Place of Birth:
Nabburg, Germany (a small town in northern Bavaria)

Current Residence:
Darmstadt, Germany (a medium-sized town near Frankfurt)

What is the best thing about where you live?

Having a spacious house and garden in a green neighborhood while enjoying all the options a vibrant city nearby is offering.

How has life changed in your country since you were a child?

In almost every respect: I grew up in a family with three sisters and the traditional role model where my mother was taking care of us full-time and my father was barely present. Today, families with four children are rare (the average "reproduction rate" being around 1.6 children), mothers tend to work, and they share the household duties with their husband.

When (and where) I grew up, there were no foreign children in kindergarten or school. Today, Germany is a diverse and multicultural society.

In the 1960s and 1970s, there was a general spirit of optimism, boosted by rising prosperity, better education (my generation was the first in the family history to graduate from "gymnasium" and study at university), progress in technology (I have never forgotten watching the landing on the moon), liberal politics, etc.

Today, the general mood is skepticism: a deteriorating infrastructure, a growing sense of declining public safety and order, waning economic strength, irregular immigration and climate change. These are the challenges that shape today's public discourse in Germany.

When I grew up, life was pretty much local. With the European Union and more immigrants, it got more colorful and international.

In our youth, we still wrote letters to communicate and often waited weeks or months for a reply. The telephone at home was fixed to a wall and if you wanted to make more personal calls, you had to go to the nearest yellow phone box with some pennies in order not to run out too fast from supply (because phone time was measured in units that cost two pennies each). But usually, you were reminded to be brief anyway by the queue of waiting people in front of its door.

Although I have integrated modern technology into my communication, I am still making phone calls while younger people hate them. They prefer WhatsApp messaging, etc.

What has been the most important event in your country in your lifetime?

The reunification of the two Germanies in 1990 — with all the ambiguities it presented.

How has your view of work changed over time?

Not so much. Not even the big step I took almost 25 years ago becoming an entrepreneur. I always loved what I did. And I always knew and appreciated that an interesting career needs effort. The only thing is that technology and changes in the media industry have increased the pace and the density of work, which is challenging to keep up with.

Tell me about your family:

As the only son among three sisters, I enjoyed some privileges that stem from the traditional role models in my parent family. That may explain why I never learned how to cook, for example.

Through my father — who was not only the local reporter for the regional newspaper but at the same time involved in local politics, honorary posts and, not to forget, his main job in a print shop — I also got interested in journalism and politics, but on another scale and with another scope. So, I left my small hometown just after school — first for the then-mandatory military service, then for university and work.

The flip side of my father's public life was that he had no time for (and I assume he was not really interested in) family life. My other parent, in contrast, was a very kind, warm-hearted and caring person who devoted her life to nurture the family. Unfortunately, she suffered from chronic polyarthritis since her early 30s, which made her late life very restricted and exhausting.

What is the most important lesson that your family taught you?
The confidence in myself and God's favor.

What's your biggest fear?
That the long period of peace we have been enjoying might end.

What is your greatest pride?
Having set up my own business, which gives me freedom and satisfaction.

What was the favorite time of your life?
The two years in Brussels as a young professional, recently graduated from university and the school of journalism, working in the press department of a European Union institution and enjoying all the convenience (money), insights (into politics) and possibilities (of a thriving and ambitious young man).

What is the best decision you made?
Marrying my wife and settling down.

Do you have a hidden talent?
Music and photography.

What advice do you have for the next generation?
Think for yourself! They should critically scrutinize everything they read or hear. In the world of new media, where ethical standards no longer apply, scrutinizing sources is crucial.

ETHIOPIA

KENYA

ZIMBABWE

LESOTHO

EGYPT

DEM. REP. CONGO

NAMIBIA

SOUTH AFRICA

NIGERIA

MOROCCO

CAPE VERDE

AFRICA

IN SOME WAYS, THE 54 COUNTRIES ON THE AFRICAN CONTINENT ARE "NEW": MOST GAINED INDEPENDENCE AFTER WORLD WAR II AS THEIR EUROPEAN OVERSEERS — MAINLY THE UNITED KINGDOM, FRANCE, PORTUGAL AND BELGIUM — RETREATED TO FACE THEIR OWN POST-WAR CHALLENGES.

THE UNITED NATIONS, founded in 1945, was in place and advocated for African nations through its promotion of equality, self-determination, and economic development. So how have the last 60 years gone?

First, in the 1960s the leadership vacuums in countries like Zanzibar, Tanzania, Kenya and Uganda were filled by rival revolutionaries. In the coming decades few countries would escape periods of coups, violence and civil wars. Rwandans and Sudanese suffered genocides in 1994 and 2004, respectively.

Second, the constitutional segregation by race in South Africa — apartheid — lasted until 1989. The dismantling of the government of the white minority included the release of Nelson Mandela, the rebel leader who had been imprisoned in South Africa since 1962. Under worldwide pressure, South African president F.W. de Klerk freed Mandela, then 72, and the two negotiated the end of apartheid. Mandela, who was revered for his "I am prepared to die" speech in 1964, would lead his political party, the African National Congress, to victory in 1994. The National Assembly then chose Mandela to be president of the new South Africa.

Third, the evolution of the independent countries and their leaders was influenced by the meddling of the Cold War superpowers until 1990. After that, other nations — China, for instance — took interest in the continent and its abundance of natural resources.

Fourth, Africa — the second largest continent on Earth — has seen its population climb from 313 million people in 1964 to 1.49 billion in 2024.

The economic forces in Africa have improved substantially. Natural resources include rubber, ivory, copper, gold, cotton, cocoa, tobacco, and diamonds.

Morocco

Hmad Abira

Place of Birth:
Tauz, Morocco (in the Sahara Desert)

Current Residence:
Marrakesh, Morocco

What is the best thing about where you live?

The best thing about where I live is my children. They bring so much joy and energy into our home, and living together allows us to share countless wonderful moments every day. Their laughter and love make this place truly special.

How has life changed in your country since you were a child?

Life in Morocco has changed significantly since I was a child. There has been rapid urbanization, improved infrastructure, and advancements in technology and education. Economic growth has brought new opportunities, while social changes have increased gender equality and youth engagement. However, some challenges like unemployment and regional disparities persist.

What has been the most important event in your country in your lifetime?

One of the most significant events in Morocco since 1964 was the ascension of King Mohammed VI to the throne in 1999. This marked a new era for the country, as King Mohammed VI introduced political, social, and economic reforms aimed at modernizing Morocco and promoting development. His reign has seen advancements in various sectors, including infrastructure, education, and women's rights, making it a pivotal period in the country's history.

How has your view of work changed over time?

Over the years, my view of work has transformed significantly, primarily influenced by the rise of social media.

In the past, work and reputation were largely shaped by direct interactions and word-of-mouth. Your professional image was built through personal connections, recommendations, and face-to-face networking. Success relied heavily on the quality of your work being relayed from one person to another. However, with the advent of social media, the landscape has dramatically shifted. Today, our professional presence and reputation are often defined by our online activities. Social media platforms like LinkedIn, Twitter (now X), and Instagram have become vital tools for showcasing skills, achievements, and thought leadership. This visibility can reach a global audience, far beyond the immediate circle of colleagues and clients we traditionally relied upon.

Tell me about your family:

I was born in a nomadic tent in the vast expanse of the Sahara Desert. My family has deep roots in this region, embracing the nomadic lifestyle that has been passed down through generations.

My mother, a resilient and adventurous woman, crossed the border into Algeria, where she got married and had two children. After her divorce, she demonstrated remarkable strength and determination by traveling back to Morocco with nothing but a donkey for transportation.

Upon returning to Morocco, my mother met my father, and together they built a life for us in the same desert that had always been our home.

We are a family of six: two brothers and two sisters. Growing up, we embraced the challenges and beauty of the nomadic lifestyle, living in a tent that moved with the rhythms of the desert.

Our childhood was a blend of adventure and simplicity, filled with the unique experiences that come with living in one of the most iconic deserts in the world.

We learned to appreciate the vast landscapes, the star-filled nights, and the sense of freedom that came with our nomadic way of life. Our upbringing in the Sahara Desert has profoundly shaped who we are, instilling in us a deep connection to our heritage and the land we call home.

My journey began at the tender age of 11, when I found myself assisting tourists stranded in the vastness of the Sahara Desert. It was there, amidst the golden sands and shimmering heat, that I learned the value of resourcefulness and hospitality. With each tip earned from guiding lost travelers, I took steps towards a brighter future.

Soon, I ventured into selling fossils to those captivated by the ancient treasures of the desert. The trade flourished, propelling me from a humble bike to a roaring motorcycle and eventually to the ownership of a car. But it wasn't just about the vehicles; each acquisition symbolized progress, independence, and the promise of greater things to come.

Then fate intervened in the form of a partnership with a German colleague. Together, we embarked on a venture that would transform our lives. Shipping tons of fossils from the Sahara to Germany opened up avenues of financial stability and opportunities previously unimaginable.

With newfound prosperity, I seized the chance to reunite my family under one roof. The decision to construct a home in Erfoud City, a testament to years of hard work and determination, brought tears of joy as my loved ones beheld the city lights for the first time.

Their awe at the modern amenities, from running water to electricity, mirrored my own astonishment at how far we had come.

What is the most important lesson that your family taught you?

One of the most important lessons my family has taught me is the value of unity and strength in togetherness.

Throughout my life, my family has always been my everything, a constant source of support and love. This lesson of staying compact and strong as a unit has proven invaluable as I've grown older. Now, my children, who were raised with these same values, surround me with care and support. Their presence and dedication remind me daily of the profound impact that our family's togetherness has had on all our lives.

What's your biggest fear?

As a nomadic man who has lived in the harsh and arid conditions of the desert, my greatest fear is drought and the looming threat of water scarcity that faces our beloved country, Morocco. Water is the cornerstone of all forms of life. In our modern cities, it's easy to take for granted the water that flows so freely from our taps. However, for those of us who have experienced life in the desert, the reality is starkly different.

Scarcity of water has been a constant challenge, dictating our every move and decision. We were often forced to move from one place to another in search of this precious resource, understanding firsthand the struggle to survive without it.

Living with less water means grappling with thirst, reduced agricultural yields, and the profound impact on daily life and health. It is a struggle that is becoming all too real for many Moroccans as climate change intensifies and water sources dwindle.

What is your greatest pride?

My greatest pride is undoubtedly my children. They have excelled in their education and are now thriving in the tourism industry. Together, they run a successful business called "I Morocco Tours." Their dedication and hard work are evident as they meticulously organize tours throughout Morocco, showcasing the beauty and culture of our country to visitors from around the world.

As tour guides, they provide an exceptional experience for their clients, who consistently express high levels of satisfaction and happiness with their services. It's heartwarming to see them passionately sharing our heritage and ensuring that every guest has a memorable and enriching experience in Morocco. Their achievements and the positive impact they make on others fill me with immense pride and joy.

What was the favorite time of your life?

My favorite time in life was undoubtedly when I first started working and managed to transition my family from a nomadic tent to a house in the bustling city. It was a time filled with challenges, but also with immense satisfaction and pride.

What is the best decision you made?

One of the best decisions I made was purchasing a house in Marrakesh and moving there with my children. This decision opened up numerous opportunities for us. Living in Marrakesh allowed my kids to immerse themselves in a vibrant culture and engage with a diverse community, enhancing their social skills and broadening their perspectives.

Do you have a hidden talent?

Yes, I believe my hidden talent lies in my ability to work hard and believe in myself. While this may not seem like a traditional talent, it has been incredibly powerful in helping me achieve my goals. I have learned to stay persistent and motivated even in challenging situations.

What advice do you have for the next generation?

One piece of advice I have for the next generation is to embrace change and be open to new experiences. The world is evolving rapidly, and the ability to adapt and learn continuously will be crucial for success.

Take risks and don't be afraid of failure; it's often through our mistakes that we learn the most valuable lessons. Additionally, prioritize building strong relationships and networking. Surround yourself with diverse, supportive people who inspire and challenge you. In an interconnected world, the ability to collaborate and communicate effectively will be essential.

Lastly, focus on sustainability and ethical practices in whatever you do. Be mindful of the impact your actions have on the environment and society. Strive to make choices that contribute positively to the world and ensure a better future for generations to come.

VIEW OF THE NILE RIVER, CAIRO, EGYPT

MOHAMED AHMED/UNSPLASH

Egypt

Zaki Habib Shenouda Fam

Place of Birth:
Cairo, Egypt

Current Residence:
Cairo, Egypt

What is the best thing about where you live?
The people. Nature. The moderate weather.

What is the most important lesson that your family taught you?
Cooperation and love without conditions.

What is your biggest fear?
I don't fear anything.

How has life changed in your country since you were a child?
The population increased, as did the prices of goods.

What is your greatest pride?
I accepted Jesus as my only savior. Also, working as a teacher. And guiding my children as a father.

What has been the most important event in your country in your lifetime?
The Egyptian revolution in January in 2011.

What is the favorite time of your life?
Reading time.

How has your view of work changed over time?
I see my job as a teacher continuing to be the most important endeavor through all these years.

What is the best decision you made?
Accepting Jesus as my personal savior.

Do you have a hidden talent?
Writing.

Tell me about your family:
I have been married 30 years. I have two sons, one is an engineer and the other is still studying at university.

What advice do you have for the next generation?
Come up with a good plan for life for every step and listen to advice that is offered.

Ethiopia

Wondwossen Tamrat

Place of Birth:
Hararghe, Ethiopia

Current Residence:
Addis Ababa, Ethiopia

What is the best thing about where you live?

I am living in the capital city of Ethiopia, Addis Ababa, and I am very close to all services and goods that are being transacted in Ethiopia. The standards of services and goods I am getting in the city is to the standard I need. Moreover, I am very proud for living in the diplomatic city of Africa since the African Union headquarters is located in Addis Ababa. The job opportunities are also higher in Addis Ababa than regional towns of Ethiopia. The political condition and the security are also much better in Addis Ababa than the rest of the country.

How has life changed in your country since you were a child?

Life has dramatically changed over the years. The living conditions became expensive, and culture and norms of the society have been affected positively and negatively as well. The birth rate has increased from what it was 20 to 30 years ago. The climatic conditions have changed. The technological advancement has been tremendous over the last decade.

What has been the most important event in your country in your lifetime?

The political situation was volatile over the last many decades. Ethiopia has been prone to Western political dominance. The competition between capitalism and socialism has significantly affected Ethiopia, where the poor nature of the country has forced it to muddle between West and East for their support, which has resulted in developing dependency syndrome on these nations while being ambitious to grow as well.

How has your view of work changed over time?

I was respecting every type of work at the beginning of my life but as demands grew, so did the appetite for better jobs. The norms and culture of work were very interesting at the beginning but as retirement approaches, job security and income-related issues became the priority over the jobs.

Tell me about your family:

My parents have passed away in the last decade. They were both farmers. I am a graduate and working in a non-governmental organization here. I am married and have two kids with my current wife (a daughter and a son).

What is the most important lesson that your family taught you?

My family taught me to be dedicated to work, and to love people and neighbors. They also taught me to be honest, genuine and committed to any assignment, including farming and education.

What's your biggest fear?

My biggest fear is life after my death and how my kids grow in my absence.

What is your greatest pride?

Behaving the way my parents wanted me to behave, in terms of work and education.

What was the favorite time of your life?

The favorite time of my life was when I was a shepherd and when I traveled to countries in Europe, Asia, and Africa.

What is the best decision you made?

The best decision I made was shifting work from the staff of the Sheraton Addis, a Luxury Collection Hotel, to traveling to rural areas and supporting poor farming households through employment in an environmental NGO.

Do you have a hidden talent?

Yes, writing poems.

What advice do you have for the next generation?

Respect elders, love working, avoid too much technology, be close to nature, fear God and be generous.

ADDIS ABABA, OROMIA, ETHIOPIA
ABDULLAH ALJABERTI/PEXELS

Kenya

Sammy Wamuri

Place of Birth:
Kisumu County, Kenya

Current Residence:
Nairobi, Kenya

What's the best thing about where you live?

I am proud to be a Kenyan, a country of marathon champions. Nairobi is the only capital city in the world with a national park only eight kilometers from downtown.

How has life changed in your country since you were a child?

Kenya became a sovereign state on June 1, 1963, soon after I was born. It attained its independence from Great Britain on Dec. 12, 1963.

Even after colonialism, the British ruled Kenya under cover for another 20 years, using the Indian loyalists here and our own black Kenyan people. The Indians worked as administrators under the British bosses.

Despite independence, many Kenyans were still not educated. We lacked the knowledge of finance, commerce and economics. Only the Indians had these skills.

It was about 10 years after independence when schools started to open up but there was still racism toward black Kenyans.

In 1994, my firstborn could not be admitted at Aga Khan kindergarten (the Indian Foundation School). I had to take her to Riverside Junior Academy (which was all white) but they were accommodating.

But now, Kenya's image looks real and is so much Kenyan.

What was the most important event in your country in your lifetime?

The most memorable crises are because Kenya has common borders with countries that have had rough pasts with war, like Somalia, Sudan and South Sudan, Ethiopia, Uganda, Rwanda and Burundi. Kenya has always been the buffer zone for all of them during war.

The most memorable moment in Nairobi during my childhood was when Nairobi at night was an attraction for people from all over the world. It was an entertainment city, with high-tech nightclubs owned by whites and Indians.

How has your view of work changed over time?

The most important event in my lifetime was when I was officially and publicly recognized by our local media as a *sapeur* (fashion icon). I then started the Sapology (Dandy) Movement in Kenya.

EDITOR's NOTE: *SAPE is a French acronym for Societe des Ambianceurs et Persons Elegants; or, loosely translated, the Society of Entertainers and Elegant People. Its roots go back to Congo in the 1920s, when individuals began to wear European outfits as a means to greater social stature.*

This was followed two years ago by a Sape competition in Kenya organized by the French ambassador. It launched Sape as a cultural movement in Kenya. Out of more than 20 competitors from different parts of Africa, I won the event. Sape culture is now recognized and protected by UNESCO.

This led to more opportunities. I did a Zoom meeting lecture on sapology and dandy culture for the Canadian International School students in California. Alex Postman, an American journalist working with Oprah Winfrey, came to my residence during her recent trip to Kenya to cover my story. Also, Olivia Buckingham, a Vogue fashion journalist, visited my home to see my fashion collection and my shoe museum.

I am currently working with Roar Africa as a guest relations officer in Nairobi. Working for this company has greatly and positively impacted my life. Apart from educating my family, this company has expanded my horizons.

Tell me about your family:

During my early childhood, I was adopted and educated by an Indian family. My dad worked for them as a house servant for 48 years. They relocated to Florida 20 years ago but I am still very close to them and we keep in touch.

I am now a single parent living in Nairobi with my 8-year-old boy and a house helper.

Since my younger days, life has really changed. Women have become so much more empowered that the marriage tradition in Kenya has faded away. Our women all want to be career women. It is difficult to assess who is wife material, which creates a total mess in my bald head.

What is the most important lesson that your family taught you?

My father taught me four things:

1. Respect your parents (mother/father).
2. Respect your guardian.
3. Respect your teacher.
4. Respect your employer.

And, in return, you will reap the benefits of being an obedient and respectful child.

What's your biggest fear?

Death. I would love to live forever, enjoying my fashion gear, including shoes, walking sticks, designer hats, and pipes. If it were possible, I would find someone to die on my behalf.

What is your greatest pride?

My pride is, once upon a time, a young boy from a very humble background made big strides in achieving his dream. My greatest pride is having worked for Roar Africa and Deb Calmeyer. I will forever remember her.

What was the favorite time of your life?

When my boss discovered that I love the most — this thing that I love the most — I wasn't sure what her reaction would be. To my surprise, she was delighted and has been very supportive since then.

What is the best decision you made?

The best decision I ever made was when temporarily left Roar Africa and stayed away for four and a half years then decided to return.

Do you have a hidden talent?

I am a graduate of applied linguistics. I speak fluent Italian and German. In total, I speak fluently nine different languages. At my leisure and in my spare time, I am doing research on soccer with an idea to make an invention. I know exactly what I want to achieve.

SAMMY WAMURI IN NAIROBI, KENYA
PHOTO COURTESY OF SAMMY

What advice do you have for the next generation?

My advice is to dream for a life and to pursue it to the extreme. Never believe in death; live your life to the fullest and live to tell a story. Any failure should be seen as a blessing in disguise.

Namibia

Guillaume 'Giel' Matthys Du Toit

Place of Birth:
Maltahohe, a town in Southern Namibia

Current Residence:
Lüderitzbucht, where my parents also stayed for some time after World War II and worked here on the diamond fields.

What is the best thing about where you live?
It's remote. One road in, same road out. Our strong winds "protect" us from over-development.

How has life changed in your country since you were a child?
A lot and it is frightening. There is a lack of discipline.

What has been the most important event in your country in your lifetime?
Namibia's independence in 1989.

How has your view of work changed over time?
Most corporations are evil.

Tell me about your family:
My father was born in Cape Province and the family moved to what was then South West Africa. From my mom's side, the family was involve in ox wagon transport since the early 1700s. They all got established around Maltahohe, got married and the rest is history.

What is the most important lesson that your family taught you?
To respect others.

What's your biggest fear?
Something out of my control may happen to my dogs.

What is your greatest pride?
On my own achievements in life.

What was the favorite time of your life?
Hmmm, living where I am, surrounded by the desert.

What is the best decision you made?
To quit the corporate world. I should have never started my career there in the first place. I wasted 40 years of my life.

Do you have a hidden talent?
Hehe, my cooking skills.

What advice do you have for the next generation?
Educate yourself through self-studies, establish a business and stick to your values. And that business must be small. Sell food, for instance. It's cash in the hand each day.

Nigeria

Isaac Babatunde Ayoola

Place of Birth:
Lagos Island, Nigeria

Current Residence:
Ibafo area of Ogun State, Nigeria

What is the best thing about where you live?
A residential estate with serene environment.

How has life changed in your country since you were a child?
Breakdown of infrastructure, dwindling purchasing power of the currency.

What has been the most important event in your country in your lifetime?
Hosting of the 2nd World Black Festival of Arts and Culture in 1977.

How has your view of work changed over time?
It's a necessity but with caution not to compromise health.

Tell me about your family:
A career wife and five children.

What is the most important lesson that your family taught you?
A man should start family life before age 30 to give room for investment during working life.

What's your biggest fear?
The economic situation, which is driving our children out of the country.

What is your greatest pride?
1. The grace of God that gives me the ability to cope with any situation.
2. My tribe and the culture.

What was the favorite time of your life?
My service year in Nigeria under the National Youth Service Corps scheme.

What is the best decision you made?
Taking up civil engineering as career.

Do you have a hidden talent?
Yes, teaching.

What advice do you have for the next generation?
Do your utmost best for your family, friends and community.

Democratic Republic of the Congo

Muhindo Sibahirwandeke

Place of Birth:
Shabunda (South Kivu), Democratic Republic of the Congo

Current Residence:
Goma, Democratic Republic of the Congo

What's the best thing about where you live?
God's word.

How has life changed in your country since you were a child?
There is war and insecurity.

What's been the most important event in your country in your lifetime?
Mobutu Sese Seko's reign.

EDITOR'S NOTE: *Mobutu was the second president of DR Congo from 1965 to 1971, at which time he changed the name of the nation to Zaire. He was president of Zaire until 1997, when the country was invaded by Rwanda and Uganda and he went into exile. His successor, Laurent-Désiré Kabila, renamed the country the Democratic Republic of the Congo.*

How has your view of work changed over time?
Today I'm old, but I used to fish and that enabled me to get married.

Tell me about your family:
My father was Mutaka Bunakwa and my mother was Kavira Kavita. They had 10 children. Six have died in the villages because of heavy work and old age. We remain four, with me and my three brothers.

What is the most important lesson that your family taught you?
They taught me to cultivate the fields.

What's your biggest fear?
Fear of going against God's will.

What is your greatest pride?
To have children and my wife.

What was the favorite time of your life?
When I married my wife.

What is the best decision you made?
Marrying my wife.

Do you have a hidden talent?
Farming.

What advice do you have for the next generation?
Fear God and don't include yourself in all kinds of problems.

Zimbabwe

Matsika Luckmore

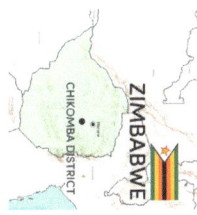

Place of Birth:
Zimbabwe

Current Residence:
Chikomba District, Zimbabwe

What is the best thing about where you live?
The Chikomba District has flat, fertile land and above-average rainfall.

What's your biggest fear?
Insecurity of my properties due to political instability.

What is your greatest pride?
Managing to produce children who are self-sustaining.

What was the favorite time of your life?
When I started to receive assistance from my three children, who are employed.

What is the best decision you made?
Buying land for my family.

Do you have a hidden talent?
Investigating cases.

What advice do you have for the next generation?
Follow your hopes and ambitions to make them fruitful.

What is the most important lesson that your family taught you?
Love and unity bring prosperity.

How has life changed in your country since you were a child?
I managed to buy land for my family and, from using the land, managed to send all my children to school.

What has been the most important event in your country in your lifetime?
Attaining independence in 1980.

How has your view of work changed over time?
I used to think that a good education and being employed were the most important things in life but now I have changed my view. Being your own master or managing your own business is the best.

Tell me about your family:
I am married to an agronomist and have five children. Three are employed in various departments and two are still at high school.

Cape Verde

Junior Batista de Pina

Place of Birth:
São Filipe, Fogo, Cape Verde

Current Residence:
Ás-Hortas, Fogo, Cape Verde

What is the best thing about where you live?

The best thing I prize about where I dwell is the company of friends and acquaintances. We do sit by the wayside and share marvelous moments.

We play cards and jest much. That's what my father did before he passed, so he perished in the pursuit of what he cherished, amidst companions.

How has life changed in your country since you were a child?

Life in our land has undergone profound changes since my youth, when we stood on the cusp of independence, having endured centuries under the Portuguese yoke. Our shores once echoed with the anguish of the slave trade, a chapter now consigned to history.

Technology, once a distant dream, now shapes our existence, rendering the old ways quaint and obsolete.

Remarkably, women now grace the professional realm, standing shoulder to shoulder with men, a testament to progress and equality in our times.

What has been the most important event in your country in your lifetime?

The most important event in our history was undoubtedly the independence of Cape Verde in 1975.

It was a profoundly significant moment for all of us, marking the end of Portuguese colonial rule and the beginning of a new era of self-determination and sovereignty for our country.

Independence not only provided us with the opportunity to shape our own future but also allowed us to preserve and celebrate our rich Cape Verdean culture in ways that were not possible before.

This event defined not just my own life but also the trajectory of an entire nation.

How has your view of work changed over time?

Over the years, my view on work has changed significantly. When I was young in Cape Verde, on Fogo Island, work was primarily about survival and providing for my family.

As time went on, I began to value not only the economic aspect of work but also the idea of personal growth and contributing to the community.

Now, at 60 years old, work is an integral part of my identity, but I also recognize the importance of a healthy balance between work and personal life.

I cherish the lessons learned and the connections made throughout my work journey, which have brought me not just stability but also a sense of purpose and gratitude.

Tell me about your family:

Our family is quite a large one. My parents had 14 children, but sadly three of them didn't survive.

My father worked tirelessly as a fisherman for over 55 years to ensure there was always food on our table. My mother was equally hardworking and attentive, managing everything with care.

The older children were given chores, and disobedience was met with punishment. We also spent a lot of time working in agriculture.

Nowadays, each of us has scattered around the world, but we all carry in our hearts the example of integrity that our father always embodied.

What is the most important lesson that your family taught you?

The greatest lesson I learned from my family, particularly my father, is that a man must work to eat. A man who doesn't work and relies on others doesn't deserve to be fed. Work is one of the most crucial aspects of a man's life, second only to family.

What's your biggest fear?

My greatest fear is losing my mother or loved ones whom I devote my life to. I recently lost my father and I value family bonds greatly.

What is your greatest pride?

My greatest pride is being born where I was born and having a beautiful, marvelous, and welcoming family like mine. I thank God every day for that.

What was the favorite time of your life?

My fondest days were when our entire family dwelt under one roof — father, mother, my 10 siblings, and myself. Those moments were priceless, beyond the reach of wealth, never to return.

What is the best decision you ever made?

Aye, the finest choice I reckon I ever made was returning to my folks' abode, where I rightly ought not to have departed, and lending a hand to my dear parents with all they required. It brought me a sense of purpose and a peace of mind that nothing else could match.

Folks around me, they love it. Family gatherings, friends' parties, you name it. I've always got a joke up my sleeve (sometimes I even cook 'em up myself, just to see those smiles light up).

It's a little thing, really, but it brings us all together, and that's what matters most in the end, isn't it?

What advice do you have for the next generation?

To the youth of today, cherish thy roots and learn from thy elders. Persevere in thy studies, be honest and diligent in thy labors. Attend to thy health and nurture strong familial bonds.

Be steadfast, contribute to thy community, and live in the present with gratitude.

Do you have a hidden talent?

Well, you see, I've got this little knack, a special talent if you will — I'm a joke-teller. Been one all my life.

PICO DO FOGO VOLCANO
FOGO ISLAND, CAPE VERDE
WIKIIMAGES/PIXABAY

South Africa

Mashudu Abednico Mudau

Place of Birth:
Venda, Limpopo Province, South Africa

Current Residence:
Johannesburg, South Africa

What is the best thing about where you live?

The area is safe and people look after each other. We fight against crime together. We have all the basic needs, like hospitals, clinics and schools.

How has life changed in your country since you were a child?

Life has changed in several ways. First, I was born and brought up during the hardest times in the country. That was during the period of segregation, where people were settled according to their color and race by force. But today people choose where they want to live, which race they want to marry from, and the system of apartheid is gone.

Today people of different races happily live together and this is a multi-racial area.

What was the most important event in your country in your lifetime?

It was when black people were allowed to go and vote in 1994 for the first time. Before 1994, black people were not allowed to vote.

How has your view of work changed over time?

My view of work has changed in such a way that it is no longer easy to find work, like how it used to be in the olden days. Too many people are competing for very few jobs.

Tell me about your family:

I am still close with my father and five siblings. My father used to work in a gold mine in Johannesburg. He also worked as a policeman until he retired in 2005. I had seven children but now I'm survived by four children — one boy and three girls. I worked as a bus driver, truck driver and most recently as a security guard. I am now retired and looking after my grandchildren.

What is the most important lesson that your family taught you?

That I should never forget my culture and heritage. They taught me to have love for the rest of the family and to respect the elders of the family.

What is your biggest fear?

That the young ones are now starting to lose focus on their culture, and it might be forgotten and erased.

What is your greatest pride?

That today I live in a free and democratic country. My other pride is that, even today, I own a piece of land in the area that belonged to our great-grandparents. I still do domestic farming and produce enough food for my family and we keep domesticated animals.

What was the favorite time of your life?

When I was a soccer star. I loved my sport very much and enjoyed it.

What is the best decision you made?
The best decision that I have made in life is to give my children education. This will help them in their entire life.

Do you have a hidden talent?
I do not have a hidden talent, otherwise I could have discovered it already.

What advice do you have for future generations?
To love and respect one another and to not forget where they come from. They must have a good education to secure better jobs and to be proud of themselves.

South Africa

Justin Stent

Place of Birth:
Pinetown, South Africa

Current Residence:
Hillcrest, South Africa

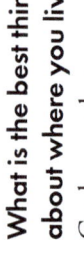

What is the best thing about where you live?
Cooler weather.

How has life changed in your country since you were a child?
Things have become difficult for all.

What has been the most important event in your country in your lifetime?
The change of government.

How has your view of work changed over time?
Fewer jobs, appointments of family and friends to high-level positions.

Tell me about your family:
My two daughters are in Johannesburg. My mom is very old and lives in Kloof. Most of the family is now overseas.

What is the most important lesson that your family taught you?
There were many things.

What's your biggest fear?
Crime.

What is your greatest pride?
I don't have a particular one.

What was the favorite time of your life?
Sailing and building cars up.

What is the best decision you made?
To start my own business.

Do you have a hidden talent?
Restoring old clocks and building gadgets in electronics.

What advice do you have for the next generation?
Study and start your own business.

South Africa

Johann Hattingh

Place of Birth:
Middelburg, Mpumalanga, South Africa

Current Residence:
Farm Keerom, Middelburg,
Mpumalanga, South Africa

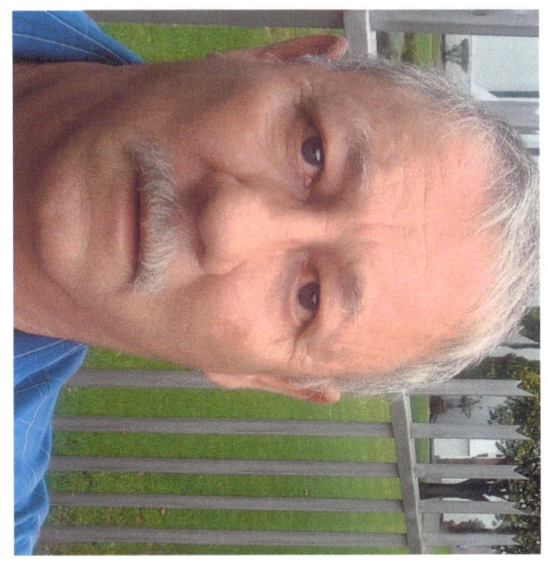

SOUTH AFRICA
MIDDELBURG

What is the best thing about where you live?
It is not a big town, which is located in the Highveld. Not too far from large cities and the capital of South Africa. It is quiet and peaceful with balanced temperatures in winter and warmth in summer.

What is the most important lesson that your family taught you?
Never stop dreaming. Take every day as a gift and be proud of who you are.

What's your biggest fear?
Losing another child. (First daughter drowned at age 2 years and 8 months.)

How has life changed in your country since you were a child?
Drastically, with the new democracy since the scrapping of "apartheid" and the new government.

What is your greatest pride?
My wife, my children and my grandkids.

What has been the most important event in your country in your lifetime?
The scrapping of "apartheid" and, of course, winning the rugby World Cup four times now.

What was the favorite time of your life?
Being a child while my parents were still alive — I miss both of them and would love to have a chat with them today as an adult.

How has your view of work changed over time?
Work is initially a punishment when you're young, but as you age you realize that it is a responsibility and a gift to be able to work.

What is the best decision you made?
Getting married a second time with the most wonderful wife. We are celebrating 20 years in September.

Tell me about your family:
Happily married with two beautiful daughters and two great sons. Best of all are my three grandchildren.

Do you have a hidden talent?
I can pinch with my toes.

What advice do you have for the next generation?
Live your dreams and believe in yourself. Be kind to others and be yourself.

South Africa

Jurg Vorholt

Place of Birth:
Sasolburg, South Africa

Current Residence:
Secunda, South Africa

What is the best thing about where you live?
The weather. Four seasons in one day :-)

How has life changed in your country since you were a child?
I grew up in the apartheid time frame. Since the early 1990s, we've been under the African National Congress government.

What has been the most important event in your country in your lifetime?
The end of apartheid.

How has your view of work changed over time?
I worked for one company for 38 years. At the end I realized that everybody is just a number.

Tell me about your family:
I've been married for 39 years. We have two children — one son with two grandsons and one daughter with one granddaughter.

What is the most important lesson that your family taught you?
To me, my family comes first. Everything else will follow.

What's your biggest fear?
Genocide in South Africa.

What is your greatest pride?
My three grandchildren.

What was the favorite time of your life?
Current. Being retired for the last two and a half years.

What is the best decision you made?
Going on early retirement.

Do you have a hidden talent?
Not that I know of. :-)

What advice do you have for the next generation?
Study as much as possible and start saving from the beginning of your career.

Lesotho

Raymond Lebona

Place of Birth:
Maseru, Lesotho

Current Residence:
Maseru, Lesotho

What is the best thing about where you live?

I have a fantastic view. I can see the trees that are along the banks of the Caledon River, which divides South Africa and Lesotho. Beyond them is a very large farmland, and in the distance hills with a blue hue. The view, at sunset, is a mosaic of greens and blues.

How has life changed in your country since you were a child?

Since I was a child, Lesotho has undergone significant changes, some good and some bad.

THE GOOD:

1. Economic development
2. Technology (mobile phones and the Internet) has helped all citizens.

THE BAD:

1. Political activities are not to the benefit of the electorate.
2. Lack of law and order.
3. Rampant fraud and corruption in public office and in the civil service.
4. Nepotism at all levels.
5. Conspicuous consumption.
6. Absence of courtesy and good manners.
7. Infrastructure has not been expanded at the same level of the economy.
8. Climate change.

What has been the most important event in your country in your lifetime?

In 1970, there was a general election in Lesotho. When the votes were counted, the governing party had lost. The result led to a coup d'état. Lesotho has never recovered from that.

How has your view of work changed over time?

When I started working, while waiting to go into tertiary education, my goal was to get a job and retire at 60. However, in the early 1990s, I became a serial "temp." The idea of working for one employer until retirement had died. My new rule was to spend no more than three years at any one position or any employer. I only broke this rule once.

Tell me about your family:

I have been happily married for nearly 26 years and I have a son.

What is the most important lesson that your family taught you?

In a nutshell, the blood of the covenant is thicker than the water of the womb.

What's your biggest fear?

Age-related diseases. I do not want to be a burden on my family.

What is your greatest pride?

My son, who will be 25 this year. He has added a whole new dimension to my business operations and my understanding of the young generation. He believes that the Millennials can teach the Baby Boomers lots of new generational tricks.

What was the favorite time of your life?

My 10 years living in London, during the 1980s and 1990s. London was the best city in the world for a bachelor, and it was at its zenith. Every nation on earth had at least one of its citizens there. I had no cat or dog. It was just me, myself, and I.

I worked hard and partied harder. I never left home without my well-thumbed copy of *London A to Z* and my Travelcard. The London Underground and London buses were my chariots.

What is the best decision you made?

In 2021, I stopped watching TV, got off the proverbial couch and started walking in early mornings. With my recently retired neighbor, whom I coerced into joining me, we would walk every day, weather permitting. We have done more than 11.6 million steps since.

Do you have a hidden talent?

In 2017, I reconnected with my creative self. I wrote a fantasy epic. It took me three months to complete the first draft. Since then, I have written novels. Creative writing is what keeps the grey matter in gear.

What advice do you have for the next generation?

You have only one life. So make it count, follow your bliss and be kind to yourself, humanity and the natural world.

MASERU, LESOTHO
TATENDA MAPIGOTI/UNSPLASH

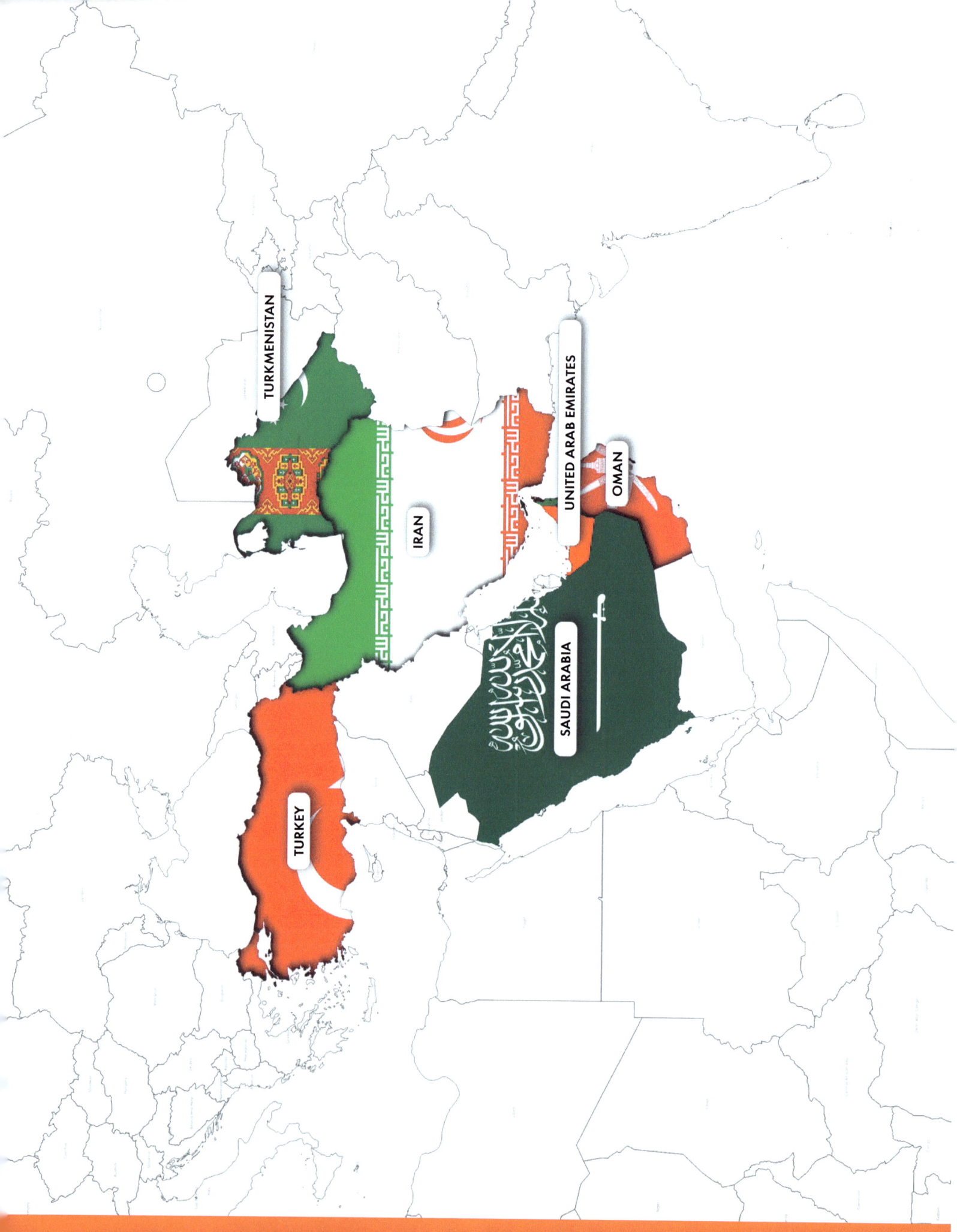

MIDDLE EAST

THE GRAND REORGANIZATION OF THE MIDDLE EAST AFTER WORLD WAR I AND THE FALL OF THE OTTOMAN EMPIRE STARTED A CENTURY OF UPHEAVAL AND CONFLICT AMONG PEOPLES WHO HAVE LIVED TOGETHER FOR THOUSANDS OF YEARS.

O NE NATION, Turkey, embraced secularism under the leadership of Mustafa Kemal Ataturk, starting in 1923. The "founding father" of the republic is revered to this day for modernizing the country and opening thousands of schools. Turkey was neutral in World War II.

The reset after that war did not quiet the consternation in the region, as boundaries were crafted to create independent states, like Israel, Syria and Jordan. Lebanon won independence from France in 1943 and the British mandate over the kingdom of Iraq ended in 1958.

The perception of the region's semi-arid desert changed, of course, with the discovery of oil in 1908. The petro economies in the region — particularly in Saudi Arabia — roared after World War II.

Revolutions, terrorism, wars and devastation came also. Lebanon, Iran, Iraq, Kuwait, Syria, Yemen — countries known more for conflict than anything else since the 1970s.

The nation that has changed the most in the last 60 years is undoubtedly the United Arab Emirates.

The main urban hubs — Abu Dhabi and Dubai — have risen from small fishing villages on the Arabian Gulf to gleaming cities of the future. Dubai boasts the world's tallest building and an assortment of "big" attractions like the huge golden Frame, an indoor ski slope, the tallest Ferris wheel, and even man-made islands created to represent the continents on Earth.

Looking ahead, this part of the world could have the most change of any region in the next 60 years.

Turkey
Ismail Yildirim

Place of Birth:
Sivas, Turkey

Current Residence:
Istanbul, Turkey

What is the best thing about where you live?

Istanbul city is home to some of the world's most famous mosques, palaces, and churches as well as being an important city during the Latin, Byzantine, and Ottoman empires. Istanbul is the only pan-continental city in the world situated on two continents, Europe and Asia.

How has life changed in your country since you were a child?

First of all, Turkey's population was 27 million in the 1960s; now it is 85 million. Due to the population increase, Turkey has been experiencing environmental pressures due to population growth, industrialization, and rapid urbanization. These pressures translate into a range of environmental challenges, such as climate change, desertification, deforestation, water scarcity, nature degradation, and marine pollution.

Nevertheless, living in Turkey is a dream of many. Turkey has beautiful natural landscapes, a rich history, delicious cuisine, an interesting culture full of unique traditions, and all mixed with a warm and pleasant climate that is perfect for living.

What has been the most important event in your country in your lifetime?

1. The Sept. 12 Military Coup or the 1980 Revolution, officially named the 12 September 1980 Operation or the Flag Operation, was the military coup carried out by the Turkish armed forces. The 45th Turkish Government — or the 1st civil government after the military regime — Özal Government was established on 13 December 1983 under the presidency of Turgut Özal. The government, which was established by the Motherland Party, served until 1987.

2. The 1999 Düzce earthquake, at 18:57 p.m. Friday. Nov. 12. The 7.5-measured earthquake with an epicenter in Düzce lasted 30 seconds and caused massive damage and casualties.

How has your view of work changed over time?

At the beginning of my career I did not have any set of the goals for the future because I just wanted to work and make some money and enjoy life and see different places. But this perspective was going to change along the way, so I did.

The first thing was that I reminded myself to take life much more seriously and set basic goals and to achieve them. I considered the best and the worst of what could happen. I observed every situation as a learning opportunity. I kept calm and controlled my composure, as I used to be a little temperamental. I tried to find the different ways to think rationally and not to jump to conclusions.

Working on cruise ships completely changed my behavior, as I had never left my country until I was 26 and began to work in such a different environment, with people from the other side of the world and from different cultures and religions. It was an important turning point in my life.

As a result, it was the biggest lesson I learned: to respect the whole Earth and humans "no matter where they came from," respect nature and respect other living things. I think the environment I work in is one of the best schools for my life.

Tell me about your family:

I got married in 1984 and have three kids. Our first daughter is now 38 and is a financial analyst in Tokyo, Japan. She works remotely for a Turkish bank. Our second daughter is 32 years old and works for the paramedic unit in the office. Our son just finished his compulsory army service.

All my children provided full support for their educations and three of them graduated from universities.

My wife is a housewife and devoted herself to look after our family, which has kept our life standard very well-managed during my absences working overseas.

I have one sister and my brother still lives with my mother, since my father passed away a few years ago. As the elder child, I keep my hands on them at all times.

According to the old and still abiding traditions, in their old age of Mom and Dad, taking care of them is one of the children's duties. It is not an alternative for us to forget the difficulties and sacrifices they have made for us while Mom and Dad were preparing us for life

What is the most important lesson that your family taught you?

Honesty, respect for the elders, loving the little ones, doing our job properly and well, not lying and not hurting anyone.

What's your biggest fear?

Invisible things, snakes and other reptiles.

What is your greatest pride?

My children.

What was the favorite time of your life?

My army service, where I formed good discipline and personality, which was the first turn of my life.

What is the best decision you made?

Investing in my children.

Do you have a hidden talent?

Home repairs and renovation work.

What advice do you have for the next generation?

Discover new ideas without bringing your old ideas along for the ride. Never reject ideas just because you will not agree with them. Examine and work on your thoughts before setting them aside. Stand out and be heard. Be respectful to the environment and to the rest of the world.

BEYAZIT TOWER *(left)* AND SULEYMANIYE MOSQUE *(right)* IN ISTANBUL, TURKEY

SAMI AKSU/PEXELS

Saudi Arabia

Ahmad Al-Akhras

Place of Birth:

Born in Libya, grew up in Amman, Jordan, and moved around. I lived in Columbus, Ohio, where I studied at the Ohio State University. I lived a few years in Abu Dhabi, United Arab Emirates, and lately I am working in Riyadh, Saudi Arabia.

Current Residence:

Riyadh, Saudi Arabia, where I am leading the effort in developing the regulatory framework for the transportation sector in one of the giga projects of Saudi Arabia.

What is the best thing about where you live?

Riyadh, the capital of Saudi Arabia, is known for its rich cultural heritage, modern architecture, and vibrant markets. The blend of tradition and modernity, along with warm hospitality, makes it a unique and dynamic city to experience. Riyadh has changed tremendously since I moved here in mid-2017. It has become more cosmopolitan and it has attracted people from all over the world.

How has life changed in your country since you were a child?

Life in Jordan has seen various changes since my childhood. Jordan has seen many technological advancements. Urban development, improved infrastructure, and increased connectivity are common aspects of such transformations. There are many things that make Jordan unique, chief among them is the archaeological, religious and tourist attractions. Petra, in the south, is considered one of the seven wonders of the world. The Dead Sea, the lowest point on earth, is a major attraction where many people have it on their bucket list to swim there and float while reading a newspaper. Wadi Rum, a desert landscape punctuated with beautiful rock formations, is very special and worth visiting. The Roman Amphitheater, smack in the heart of the capital, Amman, built in the 2nd century, is the most impressive monument of old Philadelphia, as Amman was known. Growing up, I have seen people become more appreciative of what Jordan has to offer.

What has been the most important event in your country in your lifetime?

The 1967 Arab–Israeli War, also known as the Six-Day War, had significant implications for Jordan. During the conflict, Jordan lost control of the West Bank and East Jerusalem to Israel. This loss had long-term consequences for Jordan's demographics, economy, and political stability.

Another significant event in Jordan during my lifetime was the accession of King Abdullah II to the throne in 1999 following the death of his father, King Hussein.

Additionally, the Arab Spring in 2011 led to protests and calls for political reform. While Jordan didn't experience the same level of upheaval as some other countries in the region, it prompted King Abdullah II to implement some political reforms and increase government accountability.

How has your view of work changed over time?

When I first started, work was primarily a means to earn a living or achieve financial stability. However, as I progressed, my perspective on work has broadened. I became more focused on finding fulfillment, pursuing passions, and making a meaningful contribution to society. Later in my career, I have come to value work-life balance more. I sought opportunities that align with my values, interests, and personal goals more.

Tell me about your family:

My parents played a significant role in shaping who I am and the values I hold dear. Caring, honesty, and hard work are foundational traits that they instilled in me and my siblings.

Moreover, these traits encouraged us to always self-reflect and assert accountability for ourselves and expecting it from others. These qualities contribute to a positive impact on society. My wife and I made sure that we passed these traits to our own children. We ensured that they serve as a noble source of pride. I was so proud of making a positive impact and improving the lives of others around me, especially those who cannot fight for themselves.

Another area of pride is my family, my wife and children. They represent a cornerstone of my identity and support system, providing a sense of belonging and security. Through the ups and downs of life, my family stood by me, offering guidance, encouragement, and unwavering love.

What is the most important lesson that your family taught you?

The most important lesson my family taught me is the value of love, respect, and resilience. My family instilled the three priorities in life, and these need to be in the following order: faith, family and work. If this order has shifted, the whole life will be a mess.

What's your biggest fear?

The fear of not being relevant in the world and not being able to make a difference. It is the deep-seated desire for me to lead a purposeful and impactful life. It is the concern that I may fall short of leaving a meaningful legacy, contributing to positive change, and leaving a lasting mark on the world. I try hard to cultivate meaningful connections, living in alignment with my values, and making a positive impact in the lives of others around me.

What is your greatest pride?

My greatest pride is the honor of serving my community and fighting for their rights. It was a

noble source of pride. I was so proud of making a technical skills to navigate the depths and also the ability to share my love for diving with others, instilling confidence and safety in those around me. My talent goes beyond just diving; it's about fostering a deep connection to nature and inspiring others to appreciate the beauty and wonder of the undersea's mysteries.

What was the favorite time of your life?

It was, and still is, the time I feel that I am making a difference in the lives of people around me. It is the time I volunteer to help others. It is the time when I feel a sense of purpose and fulfillment, whether through personal accomplishments, career success, or making a positive impact on others. On a personal level, it is the time where I have deep bonding with my family and friends, the moments we share experiences.

What is the best decision you made?

Marrying my wife, Hanan. We have been together for over 40 years. She is my best friend, my life companion, and my soulmate. Our commitment to each other enriches our lives. Through life's ups and downs, we've stood by each other's side, offering unwavering support and comfort. Our relationship serves as an inspiration to our children, showing the profound impact of love, respect, and mutual understanding.

Do you have a hidden talent?

I am a SCUBA dive instructor who finds solace in the sea. I love exploration, adventure, and the

underwater world. As an instructor, I possess the technical skills to navigate the depths and also the ability to share my love for diving with others, instilling confidence and safety in those around me. My talent goes beyond just diving; it's about fostering a deep connection to nature and inspiring others to appreciate the beauty and wonder of the undersea's mysteries.

What advice do you have for the next generation?

I would advise the next generation to prioritize what is important in life. Life is too short so we should plan accordingly. We should prioritize kindness, empathy, and resilience. While doing so, they should take care of their mental and physical well-being, emphasizing the importance of self-care, stress management, and maintaining a healthy lifestyle. They should enjoy doing what is right and forbid what is evil and wrong.

I would also emphasize the significance of building strong relationships, especially with family because they are the most important group in everyone's life.

Also, I would tell them that when life gives you lemons, make lemonade. That is, they need to embrace change, stay adaptable, and never lose sight of their values and integrity as they navigate the complexities of the modern world.

Oman

Nasser Ramadan Mubarak

Place of Birth:
Dhofar Governorate, Salalah

Current Residence:
Sultanate of Oman,
Dhofar Governorate, Salalah

What is the best thing about where you live?
There are modern developments all over the Sultanate.

How has life changed in your country since you were a child?
The Sultanate has changed it completely. It is a renaissance of development since the leadership of Sultan Qaboos bin Said.

What has been the most important event in our country in your lifetime?
The development in the Sultanate while preserving the surrounding environment and the Omani folklore.

How has your view of work changed over time?
With regard to work, I used to work for the Ministry of Labor as coordinator of the Director General of Labor in Dhofar Governorate. I retired and now I work as a tour guide, because I took previous courses.

Tell me about your family:
My family consists of three daughters and two sons; the eldest is a boy, the youngest is a boy, and three girls are between them.

What is the most important lesson your family taught you?
My family taught me self-reliance and not to depend on others because I grew up from divorced parents, meaning that they divorced when I was young.

What's your biggest fear?
That my children won't be able to grow up in a happy and good life.

What is your greatest pride?
My religion, Islam.

What was the favorite time of your life?
Each sunrise because it gives me hope and optimism.

What is the best decision you made?
To hold myself accountable and not to forget the existence of my Lord.

Do you have a hidden talent?
My favorite hobbies are swimming, horseback riding, painting, visual arts and tourism.

What advice do you have for the next generation?
Use self-reliance and perseverance to work in all civil and military conditions. And I will hope for you a good life.

Iran

Ali Pour Abbasi Amiri

Place of Birth:
Mazandaran Province, Iran

Current Residence:
Tehran, Iran

What is the best thing about where you live?

The nature, the history, the people.

How has life changed in your country since you were a child?

I can write a book about it! Growing up around the revolution in 1978 and then during the war between Iran and Iraq, it affected our country in many ways — economically, politically and internationally. It was the "suffocation era" in many different forms but, beside all these pressures, the beautiful part was the way people tolerated the struggle and were kind and supportive to each other. The next decade, during the 1990s, the situation began to change in a positive way. Industrial and economic growth began, international relations became better and, due to more open governmental policies, art and most cinema became more open, real and critical.

The growth continued until the time of Mahmoud Ahmadinejad. Due to a new political orientation, domestic and international sanctions became the main barrier toward economic growth. As always, who pays the price for politician decisions? Of course, the people. Since then, an economic decline is the main concern of the country. Current conflicts in the Middle East — mainly between Iran and Israel — push the situation further toward more challenges. As you can see, you never get bored when you are a Middle Easterner.

What has been the most important event in your country in your lifetime?

I mentioned most of them in the previous question but there have been several civic movements in the past 20 years. These movements, in the form of demonstrations and protests, were toward basic rights and freedoms.

How has your view of work changed over time?

I am a mechanical engineer and MBA holder and I have been working in manufacturing and marketing since university. It's been more than a decade that I'm running my own company. The situation changes every day in my country but I still believe industrial growth could help the country.

Tell me about your family:

My family is originally from the north, the Mazandaran province, which is located between the Alborz mountains and the Caspian Sea. The basic values of my family are ethics, education, and self-care.

What is the most important lesson that your family taught you?

Everything is temporary. Showing up is the main step toward success.

What's your biggest fear?

Losing the ones that I love.

What is your greatest pride?

My country. My family. Job and educational achievements. My horses.

What was the favorite time of your life?

Time of adventures during trips both into nature or riding horses. Reading books. Spending time with people that I love.

What is the best decision you made?

My education and job. Quitting smoking.

Do you have a hidden talent?

No.

What advice do you have for the next generation?

Pay less attention to social media. Spend more time in nature. Spend more time with your family. Read books instead of spending time on cellphones. Explore the world and yourself.

This page:

NAMAKABRUD TELECABIN, MAZANDARAN PROVINCE, IRAN

MOSTAFA MERAJI/UNSPLASH

Next page:

ATLANTIS, THE PALM, DUBAI, UNITED ARAB EMIRATES

ZAKRIA AFZAL/PEXELS

that there was much work ahead to ensure the safety and security of all American citizens.

How has your view of work changed over time?

Not really. I have always had a great work ethic and have always believed that if you do your best, you will be rewarded. I embrace my career path and every step of the way played an important role in my achieving my work goals and becoming a vice president for one of the largest companies in the world.

Tell me about your family:

My wife is *Mexicana* and 10 years younger than me. I have four children, seven grandchildren, and one great-grandchild. My family all live in the Seattle area. Two children lived in Dubai from 2014–2016 and one lived here during Covid, as her classes were online. She has an offer in one of the international schools in Dubai after graduation if she chooses to work in Dubai. My father and both my wife's parents are deceased.

My son became a drug addict many years ago and continues to struggle with addiction. He is an amazing person, funny and smart, but we haven't been able to overcome this challenge to date.

In my view, if we can't get him clean and productive, he will end up in prison or dead from the drugs or violence. Very disheartening situation that I would never wish on any parent. Painful.

What is the most important lesson that your family taught you?

Nothing is more important than one's family. When we make tough decisions, we need to always consider the impact on our family first.

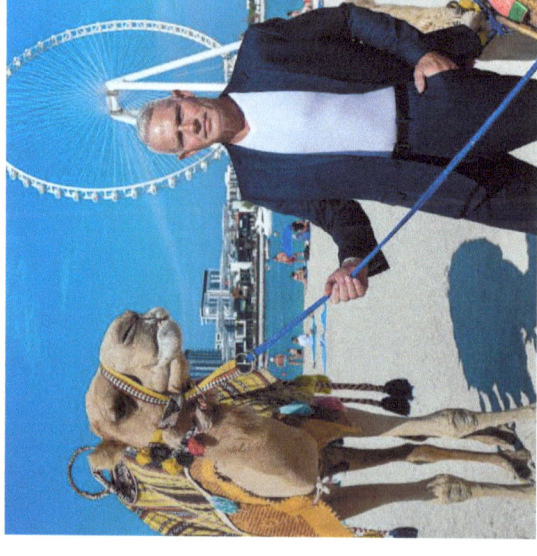

What is the best thing about where you live?

Dubai is statistically the most ethnically diverse country in the world. I have had the opportunity to make life-long friendships of persons from most countries in the world. A second benefit is that by knowing people from around the world, I also have the opportunity to learn about their cultures, religions, etc. It is amazing how such contacts open one's eyes and mind to embrace other ethnicities and cultures.

How has life changed in your country since you were a child?

I have witnessed almost incomprehensible change. I remember when my parents purchased our first television. We were all amazed, although the content was very limited. Buying my first calculator and using a computer for the first time.

Now, the challenges are with politics, as it seems as though we have lost our desire to work together in the best interest of our county. This makes me sad and concerned for the future of America.

Life is very different than it was even a few years ago. There have been struggles along the way, but life is right where I want it be and I embrace the long road it took to get here. I have much more to learn and embrace before my time is up.

What has been the most important event in your country in your lifetime?

For me, I think the 9/11 incident. It was not only tragic, but showed America is vulnerable, and

United Arab Emirates
Michael Ray Nelson

Place of Birth:
Longview, Washington, United States

Current Residence:
Dubai, United Arab Emirates

It's important not to judge family but to do our best to be there to support and love them.

What's your biggest fear?

My son dying as the result of drug abuse. It makes me ill thinking about it, which is each and every day.

What is your greatest pride?

There are many. I think my greatest pride was seeing my granddaughter and my daughter graduate from university with honors.

What was the favorite time of your life?

I have enjoyed my life from the beginning, the hard times and good times experienced. My favorite time of my life is now. I am healthy and active playing many sports, from beach volleyball, Brazilian footvolley, and skydiving. I love meeting new people and learning about cultures I was previously not aware of. Hard to beat the life we have now in Dubai.

What is the best decision you made?

I think taking this job opportunity in Dubai. My wife and I, along with our children, have all been able to experience the world at its best and worst, which has given us a different perspective on the reality of what is actually happening in the world.

We have expanded our knowledge of the world around us and learned so much about ourselves in the process.

Do you have a hidden talent?

I used to fly helicopters. Through college, I worked as a paramedic and for another 10 years after college. Loved the work, but the salary was low, which made it hard to survive. I approached a local helicopter company and made a deal with the owner to provide medical evacuation services to the ambulance company I worked with. I became good friends with the owner and eventually learned to fly. Left emergency medicine and flying to pursue my career in safety and health.

What advice do you have for the next generation?

Be patient. Take the time to learn about the world around you and embrace cultural diversity. Don't believe everything you hear on the news. Do your research before making judgments. You will learn that people who you once believed were enemies suddenly become friends.

Never stop learning. Treat others the way you wish to be treated. Always respect others' opinions and beliefs. You may not agree with them but respect them.

No matter how difficult it may be, never give up on your family. Make a commitment to attend your children's events, whether school events or sports.

Show them that they are important to you. Tell your family often that you love them.

United Arab Emirates
Johan Swemmer

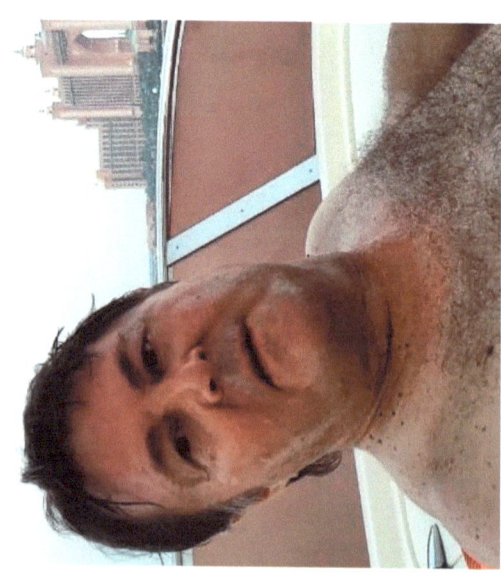

Place of Birth:
South Africa

Current Residence:
Dubai, United Arab Emirates

What is the best thing about where you live?
Everything is available (at a price) with the click of a button.

How has life changed in your country since you were a child?
Dramatically, from everything analogue to everything digital — and the politics.

What has been the most important event in your country in your lifetime?
Democracy.

How has your view of work changed over time?
Not much. Do your bit with what you have, use new tools to work smarter and be more productive.

Tell me about your family:
I have a wife, son (24) and daughter (21). We're all here in Dubai. My wife is a teacher, my son is getting ready for work life, and my daughter is studying.

What is the most important lesson that your family taught you?
They are the glue of your life; it is what keeps you together here on earth.

What's your biggest fear?
I'm not thinking about that yet. :)

What is your greatest pride?
Family.

What was the favorite time of your life?
The South African summer — sunshine and thunderstorms combined in one day.

What is the best decision you made?
There were many individual ones, adding up to bigger rewards in the end.

Do you have a hidden talent?
Many. :)

What advice do you have for the next generation?
Find your niche, find something you enjoy...and go for it!

Turkmenistan

Allabergen Rozmetovich Sapayev

Place of Birth:
Daşoguz, Turkmenistan

Current Residence:
Daşoguz, Turkmenistan

What is the best thing about where you live?

I think the best thing about the place where I live is the people. Our people are very friendly and hardworking. That's why I'm most sympathetic and inspired by my people, my folk. I believe our people are the main and most valuable resource of the country!

What has been the most important event in your country in your lifetime?

Aside from gaining independence from the Soviet Union, it was hosting the Asian Indoor and Martial Arts Games in 2017. This event elevated the status of sports in our nation. Known as "Aziada 2017," the 5th Asian Indoor and Martial Arts Games took place in Ashgabat, Turkmenistan. It was the largest international sporting event ever held in the country, with participation from 65 nations — 45 from Asia and 19 from Oceania — along with a team of refugees competing under the Olympic flag. The games were hosted at the Ashgabat Olympic Complex, a state-of-the-art facility built specifically for this event, featuring multiple sports venues, an athlete village, and other amenities.

How has life changed in your country since you were a child?

Well, I was born and grew up during the Soviet Union. Since then, both our city and country have undoubtedly progressed in a positive way.

From my perspective, I have devoted my entire life to football. I began playing as a child in third grade. Back then, we didn't have proper football fields or suitable training conditions. We essentially trained in whatever sports conditions were available.

At that time, there were only two gyms in the entire city, which belonged to sports schools. Today, with the acquisition of independence, we already have gyms in every village, collective farm, in almost every corner of the region. There are so many sports facilities and great opportunities in the region for young people to fully and productively engage in sports.

In addition, I also see how the infrastructure is developing: new, beautiful houses are being built and the city is clean and attractive. Yes, the city is transforming before our eyes. I believe that the main advantage that helped my country to

How has your view of work changed over time?

Playing sports brought me many positive emotions regarding my health. I started playing football, became a good player, played in many football teams and achieved great results. At the age of 26, I was injured as a football player and became a football referee. When I began my career as a referee, I never dreamed of becoming an international referee or a FIFA arbitrator. At that time, there were only seven quota spots available for the Soviet Union and individuals in 15 former Soviet republics were competing for them. Winning this spot seemed impossible.

After Turkmenistan gained independence, I was included in the list of international

grow and transform has been the attainment of independence in 1991.

arbitrators (the "FIFA list") and received this title. I didn't even dream about it, so I think it's one of the most significant events in my life. That's when I started officiating at international matches, Asian championships, Asian Games, and World Cup qualifiers as a part of the Asian Championships League.

In addition to my refereeing duties, I coached football teams when I had enough free time and coached junior teams of children. One of the teams that I coached became champions on the regional and state levels several times. When you start working with someone, training someone or educating someone, the main goal for them is to be good people in the end.

Tell me about your family:

I have two sons and a daughter. Both my sons and my daughter have completed higher education and are currently employed. My oldest son, who is 37, pursued a similar path to mine; he became both a football coach and referee. He trains junior teams, which show good results. My youngest son is 32. He holds a bachelor's degree in economics and he also enjoys being involved in football refereeing in his spare time. My daughter is 35 and she is also doing well and is employed.

My wife is a teacher. She worked as a kindergarten instructor for many years. Kindergarten lays the foundation for future development and much depends on the teacher and the school. I believe my wife has made a significant contribution to the education field. I have great respect for her and her profession. Without the support of my family and my wife, none of my career would have been possible. I was often away for work, traveling to many different countries around the world.

During these times, my wife became the primary support for our family, raising our children. When I was away for extended periods, I could completely rely on her. I wouldn't have achieved this stage without their tremendous support and contribution.

What is the most important lesson that your family taught you?

The primary lesson instilled by my family is the significance of unity and support. What matters most to me is ensuring that there's harmony and comfort within the household.

What's your biggest fear?

To be honest, I didn't think about it. Perhaps my fear is unfinished business, not having enough time to do something important. Every person has goals in life, and they want to achieve everything they set out to do.

What is your greatest pride?

My greatest pride is my family. I believe that without them I wouldn't have achieved anything. I'm also very proud to have represented Turkmenistan in international matches. I have never let my country down in all those matches and have proudly represented Turkmenistan both as a referee and as an instructor. My greatest achievement as a football referee is officiating in the Champions League, Asian Games, and World Cup qualifying matches.

What was the favorite time of your life?

I do love spending time with my family. Spending time with my beloved grandchildren is my favorite activity and always has been. I try to play more outdoor games with my grandchildren because I want them to be engaged in sports and physical exercise. Spending time with them and giving them my attention brings me a special feeling.

What is the best decision you made?

The question is quite complex because there have been many such decisions in life. Sometimes it's very difficult to make the right choice. The most difficult decision for me was ending my career as a football player and switching to refereeing. I wanted to continue playing football, but my injury didn't allow me to. It was tough to give up football because so many aspects of my life were connected to it.

I believe that football has given me a lot: persistence, perseverance, and resourcefulness. Thanks to this, I was able to achieve something in my life. Football provided me with the opportunity to travel around the world, meet new people, establish valuable connections, and explore many countries and their cultures. Without football, I wouldn't have had these opportunities, so I have never regretted choosing this path.

When traveling to other countries, I always tried to learn about the culture and visit different sights so that I could compare them with my own. Becoming a referee meant entering a completely new sphere with new responsibilities and work.

It was hard to switch at first, but this new experience opened more opportunities for me. Although they were different from those of a football player, it was still rewarding.

Do you have a hidden talent?

I believe that my talent lies in the ability to set goals correctly. When I took on something, I thank God it worked out. I have always had the following aim: "If you take on a task, give it your absolute best effort." I think that without special talent, without skills and without perseverance, it's very challenging to achieve good results. I always aimed high with my goals and they turned out well for me. Coming from Daşoguz, I never imagined I could reach such heights.

What advice do you have for the next generation?

"Start now. Make the most of your time, necessary steps to build and work for it, the resources, and capabilities." I can say for sure that nothing is impossible in this world. The sooner you set and achieve your goals, the more success you can attain. In my life, I've learned that everything needs to be done in its own time: education, career, and family.

The sooner a person realizes that they're responsible for their own future and takes the necessary steps to build and work for it, the sooner they can create the life they truly want. It's important not to give up, even if things don't go according to the plan. There may be various obstacles in life, but the key is to persevere and be strong enough to overcome them.

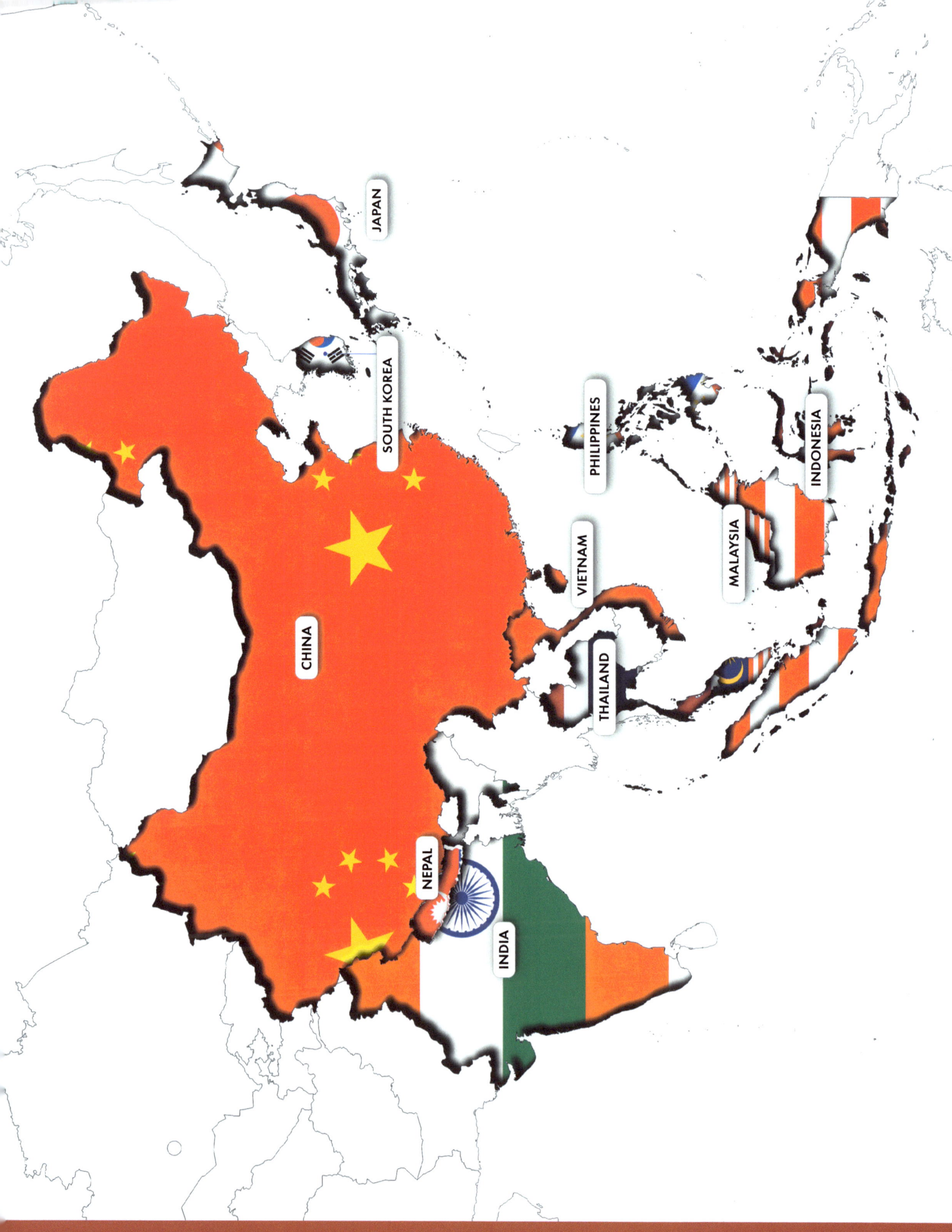

ASIA

WHEN IT COMES TO LIFE IN THE LAST 60 YEARS, THERE IS NO QUESTION THAT THE CONTINENT THAT HAS UNDERGONE THE MOST CHANGE IS ASIA.

EARTH'S LARGEST CONTINENT saw the disruption of World War II continue for another two decades, as the former European colonies seized by Imperial Japan secured various forms of independence.

Some change happened quickly — the Philippines became a republic in 1946 after the exit of the Japanese. India, a part of the British Empire since 1858, was granted its independence in 1947 by a cash-strapped British government. The British let go of Burma, now Myanmar, in 1948. The Dutch left Indonesia in 1949.

France retreated from the colonies of French Indochina — comprising Laos, Cambodia and parts of Vietnam — in 1954 in the face of nationalist uprisings. Malay, now part of Malaysia, was let go by the British in 1957. Singapore became part of Malay in 1963 before becoming its own nation-state in 1966. The British (in

Hong Kong) and the Portuguese (in Macau) held on until 1997 and 1999, respectively, when those principalities were turned over to the Chinese.

The economic surge in Asia began in post-war Japan in the 1960s. The first cars built in Japan and exported to the United States arrived in 1965. The numbers would climb dramatically in the 1970s and 1980s.

The manufacturing of electronics, textiles, garments and plastics would boost not only Japan in the coming decades but also the "Asian Tigers" — South Korea, Taiwan, Hong Kong, and Singapore.

China — closed off by Mao's destructive Cultural Revolution from 1966 to 1976 — began a massive reform effort in 1978 that reintroduced trade and marketization in the world's most populous nation.

China really exploded after a 1992 economic development initiative, which led it to becoming

the world's second biggest economy (after the United States) in 1999.

Vietnam, divided by civil war and a battleground in the Cold War for decades, saw a quick rise in incomes in the 1990s through manufacturing and exports.

As the internet spawned new enterprises, India's economy moved forward in the early 2000s through information technology. Indonesia was not far behind, with its growth spurt starting in 2007. The Philippines would follow in the 2010s.

In 1964, only two countries — China and India — were in the top 20 countries of the world in Gross Domestic Product (SEVENTH and EIGHTH, respectively).

In 2024, four countries are in the top 20 — China (SECOND); India (FIFTH); South Korea (13TH) and Indonesia (16TH).

India

Dr. Thomas B. John

Place of Birth:
Dar Es Salaam, Tanzania, East Africa. I grew up and was educated in Zambia.

Current Residence:
Kochi, Kerala, India

What is the best thing about where you live?

The perennial green environment where every neighboring tree or bush seems different to the other, coexisting — with lessons for the less-experienced human.

How has life changed in your country since you were a child?

Extended families have become nuclear families. Family prayers at the end of the day are disappearing. Neighbors are not "neighborly." Religious intolerance has increased.

What has been the most important event in your country in your lifetime?

The introduction in India of the Expanded Programme of Immunisation in 1978.

How has your view of work changed over time?

My view of work over the years has only been reinforced — work hard and from the heart! A change in my view would be possibly to understand that each member of a team has a different background, with different strengths and weaknesses. It is up to team leaders to work on these.

In addition, work is not the only thing in life. Personal health and social commitment are equally (if not more) important.

What is the most important lesson that your family taught you?

Life is short. Don't wait to enjoy family and friends.

What's your biggest fear?

Dementia. It affected my Dad, and people like Bruce Willis, Sean Connery, and Robin Williams

What is your greatest pride?

I headed a large children's department for 12 years and a newborn ICU for 20 years. My greatest pride is the professional progress made by our staff, medical and nursing. In 20 years, more than 20 of our junior doctors passed their UK post-grad exams (MRCPCH) and a large number attained consultant posts. The senior doctors attained higher positions — all in a hospital seen as a service hospital, rather than a teaching hospital.

In addition, our own children became good human beings like their Mum.

What was the favorite time of your life?

Growing up and studying in Zambia among the best people in the world.

What is the best decision you made?

When I listened to my wife and brother-in-law and accepted a job in the Sultanate of Oman for a position I thought I was too young for. This allowed me to work with and share a mentorship with a very large group of multinational medical staff from 10 different countries: Oman, India, Pakistan, Bangladesh, Sudan, Egypt, Syria, Iraq, Palestine, and the Philippines.

Do you have a hidden talent?

Ahh, it's hidden. It's the ability to speak English with the accents of different nationalities across the world.

What advice do you have for the next generation?

Strive to become a social-minded, responsible human being with responsibility for the poor, the weak, and the environment.

India

Hoshang Chothia

Place of Birth:
Mumbai, India

Current Residence:
Pune, India

What is the best thing about where you live?

Not a major city, so less traffic (relatively), better weather, affordable living.

How has life changed in your country since you were a child?

With the growing population, it has become more competitive. Things have become hugely expensive, but at the same time affordability has improved.

What has been the most important event in your country in your lifetime?

Since India's independence in 1947, one party led the government for 54 years — some years with a majority of seats and some years with a fragmented coalition government. We definitely made progress during that tenure but at the same time corruption increased and inflation grew.

Since the new government led by the Bharatiya Janata Party came to power in 2014, things have been gradually improving. There is a focus on infrastructure development, the currency has remained relatively steady over this period, corruption has been reduced to some extent, and governance has become more transparent.

India's talent pool has contributed significantly to the global economy at large and you see a lot of Indians around the globe in high-tech jobs and at the helm of major global organizations. The impact of technology has changed our lives and the Indian contribution to that is equally significant.

In my opinion, the global view of India has significantly changed and I am proud of that.

How has your view of work changed over time?

Work culture has changed a lot. The younger generation looks for work/life balance and is willing to hop jobs easily, rather than the old-school guys who were more attached to their jobs. The value for money has been reduced.

Tell me about your family:

Married, two kids, a boy and a girl, both students.

What is the most important lesson that your family taught you?

Relationships and values are more important than money.

What's your biggest fear?

Life is too uncertain. You never know what can happen in the next moment.

What is your greatest pride?

Having fulfilled my duties towards my parents, family, and country.

What was the favorite time of your life?

Relaxing at home and having fun with my school friends.

What is the best decision you made?

I decided to work in Europe for a few years and then returned back to India, thereby enjoying both worlds.

Do you have a hidden talent?
If I knew, it cannot be hidden. But, yes, I didn't know that I could paint and sing until I was 50.

What advice do you have for the next generation?
Don't be too materialistic.

MANDAI MARKETPLACE, PUNE, INDIA
ATHARVA TULSI/UNSPLASH

Nepal

Krishna Prasad Dawadi

Place of Birth:
Ajirkot, Gandaki Province, Nepal

Current Residence:
Kathmandu, Nepal

What is the best thing about where you live?

I like the place where I live because as soon as I wake up in the morning, I can see the temple of Swayambhunath on one side and the Himalayan mountains on the other side. The forest has clean air, drinking water, hospitals, schools, transportation, banking services, a clean environment and good management of peace and security.

How has life changed in your country since you were a child?

The revolution of 1989 established democracy in the country. The widespread changes brought press freedom and communication advancements that have significantly raised awareness levels. Changes such as women's empowerment, improvements in health care, the construction of rural roads, and an emphasis on human rights and the educational system have raised the standard of living.

However, during the Maoist insurgency from 1995 to 2006, several teachers and respected individuals were attacked and murdered in villages, forcing others to flee. Today, thousands of houses in villages are almost deserted, the land lies barren, and the trend of migrating to cities has rapidly increased. Many youths are engaged in foreign employment.

Students studying in village schools are rare. The sense of disintegration in village communities is palpable.

What has been the most important event in your country in your lifetime?

Democracy was established in the country by the revolution of 1989. A new constitution was enacted in 2015. The country's three-tier general elections have been held on schedule.

How has your view of work changed over time?

Many people now have access to mobile phones. Even in rural areas, it's easy to meet someone through Google. This enables people to be informed about various global issues. Machinery tools have widened the scope of work. People are actively transitioning from traditional farming and animal husbandry to other businesses.

Tell me about your family:

I have an older brother and a younger sister. I lost my mother at age 7. My father remarried and I have a brother and a sister from my stepmother. I am married and have a daughter and two sons. My daughter is married and lives in Canada. My older son is married and my younger son is 30 and single.

I lost my father in the earthquake of 2015 and my stepmother last year.

What is the most important lesson that your family taught you?

My home, family and society taught me many things. Things learned, seen and experienced during childhood are still vivid. I heard the stories of Ramayana, Mahabharata, Vishnupurana, Hiranyakasepu, demons and gods, Daitya Dhanddha, Bamha, Vishnu, Maheshwar, and the tales of Sri Swasthani.

What is your greatest pride?

1. Eighteen years ago we opened Nagarjuna Valley Academy in Kathmandu-16, as a community school. Non-profit and community-driven, this school provided scholarships to the disadvantaged, helpless, and poor students. Thousands of students have had the opportunity to study. They have become capable and have reached various heights in the world. They have contributed to women's empowerment. Society has changed. Seeing the bright smiles on their families' faces fills us with joy.

2. I explain and encourage the families of deceased individuals in society to donate their eyes for eye transplants. They donate their eyes. The world becomes visible to those who couldn't see. It makes me happy.

What is the best decision you made?

During the Maoist insurgency, we migrated. We survived. After that, we created a suitable environment to live in the society where we resided.

Do you have a hidden talent?

I love to dance to Nepali folk songs but feel shy in front of other people.

What advice do you have for the next generation?

1. Never play with people's emotions.
2. One must be patient, loyal, disciplined, and aware of their duties.
3. You must be dedicated to your work.
4. As this Earth, created by God, protects and secures our future, we must also ensure that we preserve and secure the resources for future generations, just as we strive to ensure everyone in the world lives in a suitable environment, like our precious motherland.

What was the favorite time of your life?

My childhood was exciting. From my house to the school, it took two hours crossing red soil, cutting through the forest, on an uphill road. The road was rough. Monkeys would chase me. When you come home in the evening, you are hungry and scared.

At the age of 12, I learned the English alphabet. During school breaks, my Magar friends and I used to graze the livestock in the fields of Dhodeni. We used to leave them and swim in Daroodi.

One day, our cow ate the paddy seedlings of a Thapa brother. With both hands behind my back, I was tied with a rope. They scolded me. Even my father scolded me when I came back home in the evening.

Sometimes, I would catch fish using traps, weave traps with my Magar brothers and sisters. The lessons taught by a Birini sister about catching fish, which come to water-logged fields at night after the rain, are still fresh in my memory.

In summary, I was told: "First of all, we should try to be good people." I made this my motto and have been able to survive and make a difference in a changing society.

My father used to tell me:

1. Always help the mourning family and the pregnant or new mother.
2. Never attempt suicide no matter how difficult the situation.
3. Never succumb to falsehoods and always remain loyal to the truth.
4. Learn to avoid addiction and not engage in immoral activities.
5. If you can help someone by talking and walking, do it.
6. Keep a prayer book on the pillow. It was written after many studies and discussions, so the book should be a scripture, it should be protected, and it should be read carefully.
7. Speak only after pondering the things said in the society.

What's your biggest fear?

Today, there is increasing restlessness among people in society. There is no peace. The environment of the Earth is deteriorating. Global temperatures are rising. Just a few years ago, when snow on the Annapurna Himalayas melted, people from Pokhara lost their lives due to floods. The snow in the Khumbu region is receding. There is no snow in the Himalayas. There is no water in the springs. Wildlife is facing disasters. I fear that the Earth may not be suitable for future generations to inhabit.

Thailand

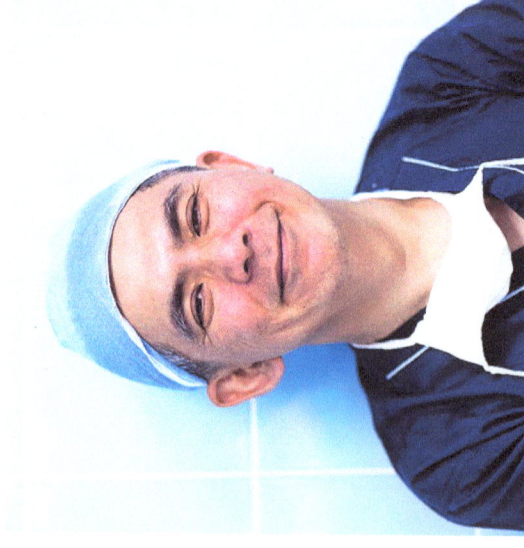

Apichai Angspatt, M.D.

Place of Birth:
Bangkok, Thailand

Current Residence:
Bangkok, Thailand

What is the best thing about where you live?

Thailand is peaceful. Although not economically the strongest country, there is no war or instability. It enables us to live happily and comfortably.

How has life changed in your country since you were a child?

Thailand has become more modernized, more convenient, more sophisticated, but also more complicated. Transportation has been one of the major changes. Back when I was young, there weren't as many roads or cars. We used boats to cross waterways and used public transportation. Bangkok was small and quiet. Now there is a lot more traffic. On top of that, for example, sending someone off abroad back then was a very big deal for the family and everyone had to be there at the airport. Now it's a very normal event. To sum up, life is easier and better.

What has been the most important event in your country in your lifetime?

The 1997 Tom Yam Kung Crisis, which originated in Thailand and led to the Asian financial crisis. We learned a lot of lessons from that event. I remembered that I went out to eat with my wife multiple times during that period and in all of the restaurants we went to, we were the only table. It was worse than Covid.

Thailand ran out of reserves. I think the Thai baht rose from 25THB per USD to 54THB per USD overnight. Apart from the above, I just feel

very lucky that we have never been through a civil war. It would have had long-term effects on our economy.

How has your view of work changed over time?

Post-graduate: 10–20 years of work — I focused on career advancement, on sharpening my academic and professional expertise, and, of course, on income. But I also followed the career path that felt meaningful to me. That was why I became a reconstructive plastic surgeon and also volunteered to do free reconstructive surgery since the beginning of my 30s.

The 20–40 years of work — Later in my career, I focused on the training of the young generation and on keeping up with new medical technologies. The medical field has changed a lot. Research has become very accessible and innovations are adopted very fast.

Tell me about your family:

We live in a very old-fashioned and large family (an extended family — Chinese style). We have been living together in one big neighborhood ever since we were children and had to share everything. It has taught us the meaning of harmony and cooperation. We became forgiving and considerate.

What is the most important lesson that your family taught you?

Unity is strength.

What's your biggest fear?

Brutal capitalism because it will increase segregation. But luckily Thailand's politics are not like this.

What is your greatest pride?

We have transformed the medical profession and the public health industry in Bangkok. Now it is one of the best in the world. Thailand is now a medical hub where patients are able to get international-standard medical services but with much lower fees.

What was the favorite time of your life?

My childhood — living with cousins, 12 of them under one roof. It was hectic but so much fun.

What is the best decision you made?

The decision to stay together as an extended family (in the same neighborhood). We all first tried splitting up, living in individual homes, but we came back.

Do you have a hidden talent?

I think maybe persuasion because I find myself as the mediator most of the time. The key is to focus on the subject and not the person. The disagreement usually doesn't stem from the topic of discussion, but from the emotions or languages involved.

What advice do you have for the next generation?

To study Buddhism because it is the learning of oneself. It teaches you to cut out greed and desire stimulators (for example, social media), which cause unhappiness and/or depression. To keep peace of mind, you should avoid all the stimulators.

CHINATOWN, BANGKOK, THAILAND
JAKOB OWENS/UNSPLASH

Singapore
Jimmy Pascal Yip

Place of Birth:
Singapore

Current Residence:
Singapore

What's your biggest fear?
Sudden death.

What is your greatest pride?
My wife and son.

What was the favorite time of your life?
My retirement, where I can spend time and travel with my family without having work on my mind.

What is the best decision you made?
To save enough for early retirement. Life is more than work and money. To retire late means one has less time left to enjoy their life or pursue what they have always wanted to do. Our body and mind age faster than we expect

Do you have a hidden talent?
I am a very witty person who can make people around me relax and laugh over my jokes.

What advice do you have for the next generation?
Academic achievement will not define your life. I recommend learning to deal with all kinds people for survival; giving — rather than taking — to earn trust and friendship; learning as much as you can; taking on challenges outside your comfort zone; traveling as much as you can to witness and experience different cultures; and, lastly, having a spiritual life.

What is the best thing about where you live?
Security and a stable government.

How has life changed in your country since you were a child?
The cost of living has definitely gone up many folds. There are also more foreign workers, immigrants and new citizens. Many older buildings have given way to new ones. The transportation infrastructure has been given an entire face-lift with the introduction of mass transit trains (underground tubes) and modern bus fleets being regularly upgraded. People are more tech-savvy, keeping in pace to the new digital age.

What has been the most important event in your country in your lifetime?
The passing of our founding father, the late prime minister, Mr. Lee Kuan Yew, in 2015.

How has your view of work changed over time?
Digital advancement has changed the general working environment across all industry. Keeping pace can be challenging for some. One needs to level up to remain relevant in the industry.

What is the most important lesson that your family taught you?
Never forget your roots. There is no shortcut to success. Nothing beats working hard and working smart.

Singapore

Noor Hassan

Place of Birth:
Singapore

Current Residence:
Singapore

What is the best thing about where you live?
Being near nature such as creeks, vegetation and park connectors.

How has life changed in your country since you were a child?
Cleaner public housing.

What has been the most important event in your country in your lifetime?
The upholding of education standards.

How has your view of work changed over time?
Work has gradually improved and it is easier to perform, due to automation.

Tell me about your family:
There are four of us — my wife, my daughter and my son-in-law.

What is the most important lesson that your family taught you?
Self-discipline.

What's your biggest fear?
Poverty.

What is your greatest pride?
Humility.

What was the favorite time of your life?
Running my family.

What is the best decision you made?
Getting married.

Do you have a hidden talent?
Singing.

What advice do you have for the next generation?
Treasure your family.

ROOFTOP SWIMMING POOL, MARINA BAY SANDS HOTEL, SINGAPORE

©NJARVIS5/DREAMSTIME

Malaysia

Khoo Boo Lim

Place of Birth:
Penang, Malaysia

Current Residence:
Batu Feringgi, Penang, Malaysia

What is the best thing about where you live?

It is a tourist resort town that has many wonderful hotels with the best beach in Penang.

How has life changed in your country since you were a child?

Penang has changed from a sleepy, laid-back island to a bustling city. Tourism and manufacturing have played major roles in that evolution.

What has been the most important event in your country in your lifetime?

I guess it was the time when the longest ruling political party (for more than 61 years), the United Malays National Organisation (UMNO), lost in the 14th General Election in 2018.

How has your view of work changed over time?

The most significant area of change I would say is the technological enhancements. It definitely changed the way we work and the way we do business. I am in the hotel industry; I must admit that technology has changed the way we operate a hotel, except for the human touches that are irreplaceable when dealing with a guest.

Tell me about your family:

I come from a working-class family. My father was a storekeeper and my mother a housewife. I have one eldest sister, who has migrated to Australia, and an elder brother, who has passed on. I still have my second brother and a younger sister around. As for my own family, my wife is of the same age as myself and we have two children, a daughter, 32, and a son, 29.

What is the most important lesson that your family taught you?

I think the greatest influence in our family was our mother. She is a strong woman who sacrifices everything for her children. She is a strong advocate of education and perseverance in achieving your goals in life.

What's your biggest fear?

Avoiding any major illness.

What is your greatest pride?

Being recognized by the state government for my contributions to the tourism industry of Penang. I was awarded a State Award, which carries the title "Dato."

What was the favorite time of your life?

School days!

What is the best decision you made?

To change my working career during mid-life from electronics to hospitality.

Do you have a hidden talent?

I guess I would have been a great chef!

What advice do you have for the next generation?

I hope the new generation will be more resilient and be able to face life's challenges with more calmness and responsibility.

Malaysia
Tan Seang Aun

Place of Birth:
Penang, Malaysia

Current Residence:
Island Park, Penang, Malaysia

What is the best thing about where you live?
There is a beautiful garden with a river running through with two small bridges, known as a mini Japanese garden.

How has life changed in your country since you were a child?
We are a modernized country with many new, tall and modern buildings, compared to the 1970s. I do miss the old hawkers' food, which no longer exists. Tastes have changed over the decades.

What has been the most important event in your country in your lifetime?
The change of the Penang state government in 2008, when the opposition won and took over from the ruling state government.

How has your view of work changed over time?
Work has changed, especially in information technology. It is fast-moving and makes work more efficient.

Tell me about your family:
My father has passed away. I am now with my mom and sister.

What is the most important lesson that your family taught you?
Honesty, being humble, respect and manners to all.

What's your biggest fear?
Sickness, as health is wealth.

What is your greatest pride?
Becoming the chief executive officer of a private hospital is an achievement in my career.

What was the favorite time of your life?
Traveling overseas for work in Singapore, Thailand, China, Vietnam, Indonesia and Spain.

What is the best decision you made?
My decision to switch careers. I changed from manufacturing/construction to top management in the healthcare/hospital industry.

Do you have a hidden talent?
A strong willpower and positive mindset.

What advice do you have for the next generation?
Be honest and humble to all and dare to take on challenges.

South Korea

Lee Ae-hong

Place of Birth:
Geochang-gun,
Gyeongsangnam-do, South Korea

Current Residence:
Seoul, South Korea

What is the best thing about where you live?
Being able to watch the sunrise and sunset over-looking the Han River.

How has life changed in your country since you were a child?
The fast economic growth that amazes the world.

What was the most important event in your country in your lifetime?
The assassination of President Park Chung Hee in 1979 and the democratization movement that followed in 1980. Other highlights were the Olympic Winter Games in 1988 and the FIFA World Cup football championship in 2002.

How has your view of work changed over time?
I used to work 16 hours a day with sleepless nights to pursue my goals, but now I take my time and pursue hobbies, letting go of my impatience with work and living a satisfying life.

Tell me about your family:
I have my parents. My mom died eight years ago. I have two sisters and one brother. My older sister lives in United States with her family; my younger sister and brother live in Korea. Also, I have four siblings and two other siblings from international marriages in the United States. They are successful in their own right. I have a 30-year-old daughter.

What is the most important lesson your family taught you?
You can't live without love.

What is your biggest fear?
Health. I am working hard to keep fit and healthy.

What is your greatest pride?
Meeting and living with my foreign wife.

What was the best time of your life?
The current time. Still in progress!

What was the best decision you made?
Getting married.

Do you have a hidden talent?
Writing poetry.

What advice do you have for the next generation?
Unlike other countries, Korea has a culture of having good manners. We value courtesy, working hard in our respective fields, loving our country, and living in peace without discrimination between people.

SUNSET OVER SEOUL, SOUTH KOREA

FELIX FUCHS/UNSPLASH

Vietnam

Minh Duy Nguyen

Place of Birth:
Dai Luong Village, Thai Hoa Commune, Vietnam

Current Residence:
Dai Luong Village, Thai Hoa Commune, Vietnam

What has been the most important event in your country in your lifetime?

Our country has gone through many ups and downs in history.

1975 was the year our country achieved complete independence and reunification, opening a new chapter of freedom and moving forward to build socialism. This was the happiest period, as it was the moment our entire nation gained independence after thousands of years of fighting against invaders.

Overcoming the hardships after the war were the years of my childhood. Growing up and starting a family coincided with the time when our country was implementing *Doi Moi* (renovation) policies, although there were many mistakes and difficulties, leaving us without jobs and life hadn't truly changed yet.

From 1986 until now, our country has continuously changed.

With multilateral cooperation with most countries in the world, it has brought jobs and improved people's lives. People's lives are becoming more prosperous and happy, and society is developing to a new level, with many century-long construction projects and numerous high-rise buildings in big cities bringing civilization and modernity.

How has your view of work changed over time?

My perspective on work has transformed throughout my life. Initially, it was about providing for my family during challenging times. Most jobs involved communal efforts, working together, earning points, and ensuring fairness for everyone — contributing and benefiting together. This was the spirit of reform during the subsidy period.

Later, when the subsidy system became outdated, we started having more jobs and focused on developing the country. Opening up and integrating with the world brought many job opportunities, more factories and businesses, joint ventures, foreign-invested companies, and large corporations investing in the country. We transitioned from being farmers and focusing on agriculture to industry and services. Many new professions emerged, and incomes gradually became more stable.

I've experienced various jobs, including being a farmer, carpenter, traditional musical-instrument maker, construction worker, and businessman. Now, in my old age, my current job is fish farming. Although the income isn't high, it's enough for me to eat and live a happy and healthy life every day.

What is the best thing about where you live?

The peace. There are no natural disasters, floods, or wars.

How has life changed in your country since you were a child?

It has changed a lot since I was born. Many high-rise buildings have sprung up, there are many new factories and businesses, people's lives are prosperous and happy, and the level of education is high. My outlook on life has completely changed, from the way I live and work, to my innovative thinking.

Tell me about your family:

My current family consists of four members. My parents passed away a few years ago at the age of 90. I am very proud of them. I have a kind and devoted wife and two sons, aged 36 and 31. They are all well-educated and have graduated from college or university. They are also successful in their own careers and very filial to their parents. I live surrounded by relatives, and everyone is happy, cheerful, and always willing to help each other.

As I've grown old, what I long for is to have grandchildren and to live peacefully in my homeland.

What is the most important lesson that your family taught you?

To live with a mindset of innovation and change, and to adapt my way of living within my family.

What's your biggest fear?

Losing the happy family that I've spent my whole life building.

What is your greatest pride?

Having a culturally rich family that meets standards. Raising well-behaved children who achieved academic success, grew up, and are fulfilling their dreams in life.

What was the favorite time of your life?

Whenever I gather with my family.

What is the best decision you made?

To fulfill my dream of having a spacious house. My children are well-behaved, successful, and have stable jobs.

Do you have a hidden talent?

I have the talent to do many jobs that require meticulousness. In particular, I have the ability to lead my family. My wife and children all know how to listen, which creates a happy family that serves as an example for society to follow.

What advice do you have for the next generation?

Live responsibly towards your family and society, have goals in life and strive wholeheartedly to achieve them.

China

Wei Xu

Place of Birth:
Village of Hubei, China

Current Residence:
Hangzhou, China

What is the best thing about where you live?
Hangzhou is a beautiful city with lots of job opportunities.

How has life changed in your country since you were a child?
We had to go to the cities to find jobs since we had nothing to do in a small, poor village. We even did not have enough food. All the young people moved out of the village; only the seniors stayed.

I did not have a chance to get an education, but I worked hard, and my life changed a lot. I have a job and I have a home. I raised two kids. Now everyone has a much better life. Some people went back to the small village and built new houses; they enjoy the retirement life there. There were not too many trees in the small village since we cut the trees and used the wood for heating or cooking before. Now there are too many trees since we only use gas or electricity.

What has been the most important event in your country in your lifetime?
The Chinese economic reform plan in 1978. We started to have the chance to work in the city.

How has your view of work changed over time?
I was working hard, not smart. Then I realized that I needed to learn some technical skills so that I could earn more money.

Tell me about your family:
I was born in a poor family in 1963. I have seven siblings; we did not have enough food when I was little. Now I have a wife and two kids. We are not rich but we still have a safe and good life.

What is the most important lesson that your family taught you?
I was taught to be honest, kind and to work hard. After so many years of hard working, I can handle any tough jobs.

What's your biggest fear?
I don't have good insurance and pension; I spent most of the money on raising kids. I am afraid that I won't have enough money to pay medical bills when I am old and sick.

What is your greatest pride?
I raised my two kids well; they received a good education and both have good jobs now. The kids don't have to repeat my hard life again.

What was the favorite time of your life?
When I sent the kids to college.

What is the best decision you made?

I spent too much time and money for kids before. I realized that I need my own life and kids need space, too. Now the kids have their own life and they are doing well. My wife and I have our own life.

We don't bother the kids too much, and we saved money for ourselves.

Do you have a hidden talent?

No.

What advice do you have for the next generation?

Young people do not work hard and they spend too much time and money on something useless. I would like to suggest that young people should focus on work and build a good life for themselves.

Japan

Fuyuhiko Hayashi

Place of Birth:
Amagasaki City, Hyogo Prefecture, Japan

Current Residence:
Toda City, Saitama Prefecture, Japan

What is the best thing about where you live?

The best thing about my city is that it is only 15 minutes by train from Ikebukuro, the sub-center of Tokyo, but it has so much nature and parks that it is called an "oasis city full of water and greenery." That's it.

How has life changed in your country since you were a child?

When I was a child, Japan was in the middle of a period of high economic growth, and the idea that everyone was the same was emphasized. After that, when the bubble economy burst and wages did not rise, I think people's lives changed to one where they valued differences and that each person's values were important.

What has been the most important event in your country in your lifetime?

In 1989, Emperor Showa passed away and the era name changed from "Showa" to "Heisei." I felt that times were changing. At that time, I went from Osaka to the Imperial Palace in Tokyo to write a book in order to express my gratitude to His Majesty the Emperor, who had passed away, and to pray for his repose.

How has your view of work changed over time?

I became a city council member seven years ago. I began to feel joy in being involved in the future of the city, nurturing local children, and working to create happiness for people.

Tell me about your family:

My ancestors lived in Gion, Kyoto, and ran a fruit and vegetable business for generations. The head of the family continues to run the family business in Gion. Our family was split up by my grandfather, who took over the fruit and vegetable business, but my father became an office worker at Sumitomo Life Insurance Co., where he met and married my mother.

My mother's ancestors ran a kimono business near Ise Jingu Shrine in Mie Prefecture, which continues to this day. Kyoto and Ise are known as historical cities in Japan. I was born as the eldest son of parents who grew up in a place where I could feel this ancient culture. The reason why I work in politics and care deeply about Japan may be because the blood of my ancestors flows through my veins. Currently, my parents are in a nursing care facility in Fukuoka City, Fukuoka Prefecture, and I share the house with my younger brother.

What is the most important lesson that your family taught you?

Passing on your thoughts will strengthen your will to live life. I learned that from my mother. Although I lost my mother at a young age, I believe that I was able to overcome the many hardships that followed because I inherited her thoughts.

What's your biggest fear?

To die without giving anything back to the world.

What is your greatest pride?

I have always had the desire to be involved in creating an environment where people can be happy, and I have actually done that kind of work.

What was the favorite time of your life?

Gaining new discoveries and wisdom through listening to other people's stories and reading books.

What is the best decision you made?

I decided to quit my previous job and become a city council member.

Do you have a hidden talent?

If I have a hidden talent, I think it might be that I can easily see through the essence of things.

What advice do you have for the next generation?

You will be able to think that all the good and bad things in life were necessary experiences in life. We all don't know what the future holds, but when we look back, we realize that everything is connected. No matter what situation you're faced with, I think it's important to move forward and think, "It's going to be okay" and "I'm sure we'll make it through."

YASAKA SHRINE, GION, KYOTO, JAPAN
WILLIAN JUSTEN DE VASCONCELLOS/UNSPLASH

Japan

Hideo

Place of Birth:
Osaka, Japan

Current Residence:
Tokyo, Japan

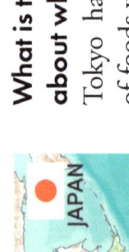

What is the best thing about where you live?

Tokyo has a wide variety of foods with good quality. Tokyo has more Michelin Star restaurants than any other big city in the world.

How has life changed in your country since you were a child?

Japan became more international. I did not have a chance to talk to foreigner until I was 17 years old, although I live in the suburb of a big city. The first time I went abroad was when I was 18 years old.

Now we see foreigners everywhere and kids travel abroad when they are small. In the 1960s and 1970s foreigners were not so interested in Japan and Japan was not respected. Now they love Japan. They like the Japanese automobiles, high-tech products, anime, zen, and other parts of our traditional culture. Japan is more respected than when I was a kid.

What has been the most important event in your country in your lifetime?

The Great East Japan Earthquake in 2011. This is because something we only see in the fiction did happen, including 30-meter-high tsunami and a nuclear-power plant accident. We became united to support the tsunami-affected areas. That was the first time, in my lifetime, a massive number of volunteers visited a disaster area, including me.

How has your view of work changed over time?

When I started my career, being successful in the company and being promoted was more important than a life/work balance. The workplace was very competitive and everyone was working very hard. I retired from the bank last year and now I am a licensed tour guide. I love to travel around Japan and I love to entertain foreigners so I really enjoy my job now. I made my hobby a job. Now I don't need to balance life and work.

Tell me about your family:

I have a wife and a grownup son and daughter.

What is the most important lesson that your family taught you?

"Do the right thing."

What's your biggest fear?

In the future, AI (artificial intelligence) may become so sophisticated and take over human beings.

What is your greatest pride?

I started my second career as a licensed English tour guide last year. I could still challenge myself and learn new things and improve myself at this age.

What was the favorite time of your life?

I love traveling by train. I enjoy a nice scenery of the beautiful countryside of Japan.

What is the best decision you made?

When I retired from the bank early and became a licensed tour guide.

Do you have a hidden talent?

I think I have an ability to take a complicated explanation and make it a simple one.

What advice do you have for the next generation?

Always think about how to differentiate yourself from others and Als and review it frequently in order to survive in the changing world.

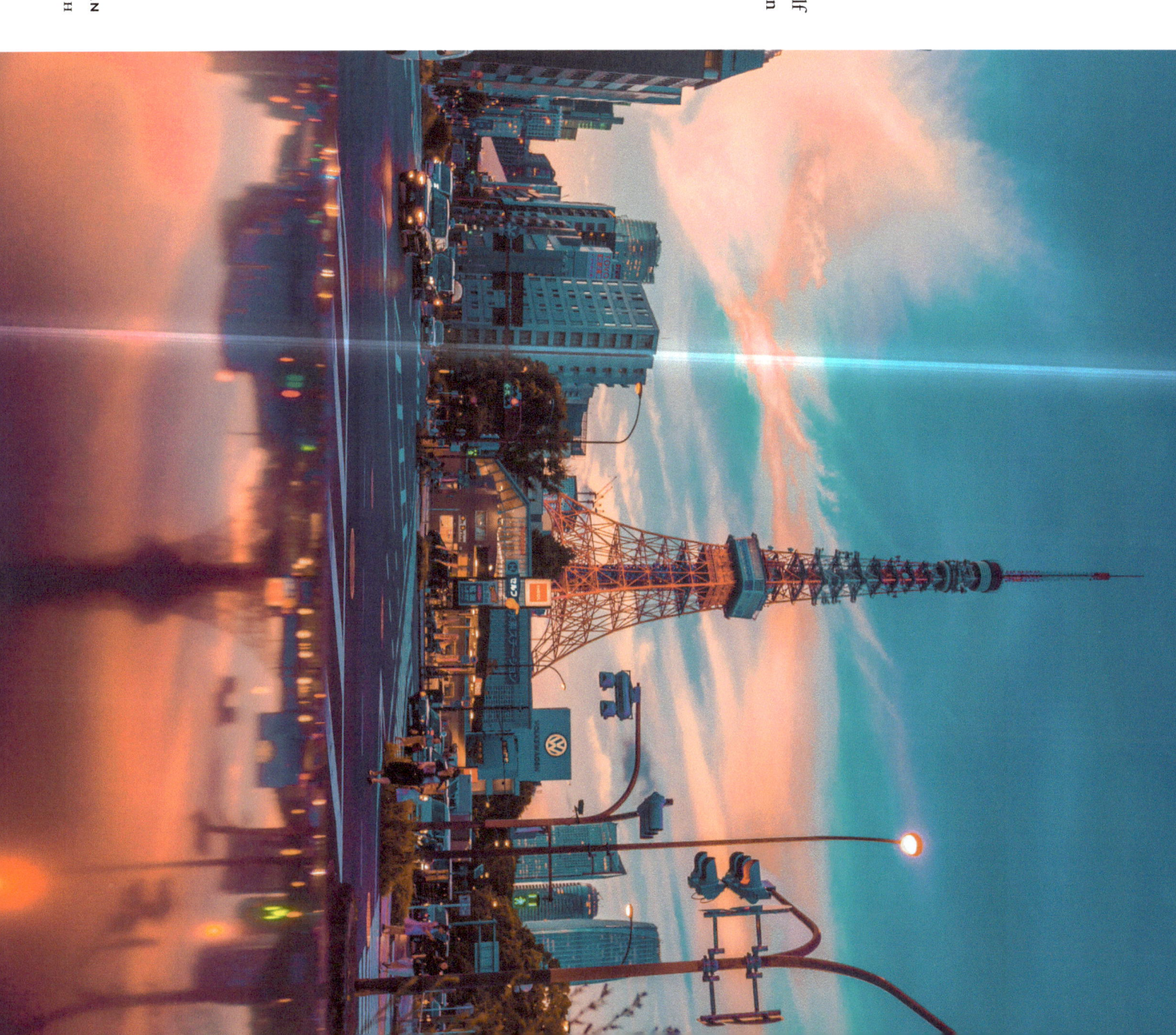

TOKYO TOWER, MINATO CITY, TOKYO, JAPAN

JEZAEL MELGOZA/UNSPLASH

Japan
Toshio Ina

Place of Birth:
Ashiya, Japan

Current Residence:
Tokyo, Japan

JAPAN

TOKYO

What is the best thing about where you live?
There is a lot of nature around us, like woods, rivers, and parks, not the sea.

How has life changed in your country since you were a child?
Society has developed much more than it did 50 years ago, and lifestyles are getting less interaction with others.

What has been the most important event in your country in your lifetime?
Making a family and the kids getting married.

How has your view of work changed over time?
As you know, we've gone from using a telephone and paperwork with a human interface to typing words on a screen.

Tell me about your family:
There is my wife and I, one daughter and one son. They have each been married recently.

What is the most important lesson that your family taught you?
Challenge yourself, enjoy and grow!

What's your biggest fear?
Nothing special, since our kids are independent.

What is your greatest pride?
I'm trying to find a new challenge and just do it right away.

What was the favorite time of your life?
The present. I am enjoying it right now.

What is the best decision you made?
Always following my inner feelings and intuition. The decisions I make were always the best.

Do you have a hidden talent?
Nothing special.

What advice do you have for the next generation?
To challenge yourself is the way to grow.

Philippines

Martin Sumulong

Place of Birth:
Quezon City, Philippines

Current Residence:
Muntinlupa City, Philippines

What is the best thing about where you live?

Living in your country of birth is always the best. We are a country of resilient people and this is very evident in times of crisis. You have the same culture and beliefs that might be difficult to understand if you were not born and raised in the Philippines.

Our country is not the most ideal place to live in but it is still what we call home. A lot of foreigners have moved to the Philippines so I guess there must be something very good about the Philippines that made them consider moving here and raising a family here.

How has life changed in your country since you were a child?

Our country has changed a lot since I was a child. Most of the agricultural land has been transformed into commercial uses. Some of the old cultures and beliefs are no longer followed by the younger generation. People tend to crowd in the key cities because most of the jobs are situated there.

The cost of living has gone up several folds. The younger generation cannot afford a house and are now part of the condominium clientele.

The sad part for me is that old values are being substituted with modern beliefs.

What has been the most important event in your country in your lifetime?

February 1986. The country deposed Ferdinand Marcos, a dictator of two decades.

How has your view of work changed over time?

Work has become more stressful. Everything is in a fast-paced mode.

Tell me about your family:

I am married with three adult children. I come from a family of four and I am the third among my siblings.

What is the most important lesson that your family taught you?

Life is hard but life is good. Perseverance is important. There is no such thing as easy money.

What's your biggest fear?

Losing my wife or any of my children.

What is your greatest pride?

My wife and children.

What was the favorite time of your life?

Nothing beats high school life!

What is the best decision you made?

Getting married and having a family of my own.

Do you have a hidden talent?

Sad to say, I don't.

What advice do you have for the next generation?

Life is a road with never-ending challenges. The important thing is to keep on moving, no matter how slow, when encountering challenges. Never give up.

Philippines
Ramon C. Calonia Jr.

Place of Birth:
Iloilo City, Philippines

Current Residence:
Molo, Iloilo City, Philippines

PHILIPPINES

MOLO

What is the best thing about where you live?
The food and the people! The city where I grew up just received an award from UNESCO as the 2023 "City of Gastronomy."

How has life changed in your country since you were a child?
Accessibility and mobility. We have a much better road infrastructure and access to vehicles for transportation.

What has been the most important event in your country in your lifetime?
The EDSA Revolution, or the People Power Revolution, in 1986, which led to the end of Ferdinand Marcos' 20-year dictatorship.

How has your view of work changed over time?
I have been more resilient.

Tell me about your family:
My son, wife and I just love living a simple, happy and peaceful life. We love spending time with our relatives by going to fiestas, which we celebrate to honor our patron saints.

What is the most important lesson that your family taught you?
Don't depend on others; be responsible and respectful.

What's your biggest fear?
War.

What is your greatest pride?
Having a degree and becoming a professional.

What was the favorite time of your life?
My son is in college so every time we are all at home together is my favorite time.

What is the best decision you made?
Being with my wife forever.

Do you have a hidden talent?
Not that I know of.

What advice do you have for the next generation?
Always be responsible and productive. Challenge myself and learn new things and improve myself at this age.

OCEANIA

THE MOST REMOTE COLLECTION OF COUNTRIES ON EARTH WAS LABELED IN 1814 BY FRENCH MAP-MAKER ADRIEN-HUBERT BRUE AS "OCEANIA."

T COMPRISES the continent of Australia, the extended country of New Zealand, and 10,000 other islands, many of which are known to travelers (Samoa, Fiji, Tahiti, Bora Bora, Papua New Guinea) but the vast majority are not. (For the purposes of this book, the resort island of Bali — which is on the eastern end of Indonesia — has been grouped with its Pacific sisters.)

There has been life in this secluded portion of the Pacific for tens of thousands of years but it was only the 1500s when Portuguese and Spanish navigators discovered the area during the "Age of Exploration." It would not be until the 1600s that Europeans set foot on Australia and the late 1700s for the British Empire to set up colonies there. Footholds in New Zealand (1840) and Fiji (1872) followed.

Today Oceania is still isolated but air travel and cruise ships have brought the region closer to the rest of the world, at least figuratively.

Every morning still starts along the International Date Line near Fiji and Samoa, when people in Japan, China, India and the Middle East are asleep and Europeans and Africans are heading to bed. Individuals in the Americas are still in the midst of the previous day.

That, plus the tropical region's location in the Southern Hemisphere, presents a distant, almost dream-like sanctuary of beaches and surf. Reality does intrude, of course. These distant islands were places of battle during World War II and saw indescribable atrocities.

The colonists who took over Australia and New Zealand were not always fair to the areas' indigenous peoples, the aborigines and the Maori, respectively. Government leaders in both countries only recently acknowledged the harm that had been done to the native populations in the previous century.

Since 1964, Oceania has been for the most part peaceful, with the exception of coups in Fiji and the Bouganville conflict in Papua New Guinea.

In fact, the largest intrusions have been by tourists, who have discovered a sunny, relaxed escape with its own rhythm of life.

Indonesia

Gusti Made Gunawan Gusti (Guna)

Place of Birth:
Tabanan, Bali, Indonesia

Current Residence:
Denpasar, Bali, Indonesia

What is the best thing about where you live?

It is close to the city center and easy to go anywhere. It gives me conveniences and comforability.

How has life changed in your country since you were a child?

There have been many changes in life since I was a kid. I was born in a small village as part of a big farming family. We lived very simple and ate whatever was available. Meats were only available in a special occasion, like a temple ceremony or wedding.

I spent my childhood with friends and played kite, fishing and traditional games during the full moon because we had no electricity yet. I went to school with bare feet, about three kilometers back and forth, and had only one uniform for the whole week. I washed it every Saturday afternoon. When I was 13 years old, my grandfather sent me to the city to continue my studies until I graduated from a college in Denpasar. I came back to the village when there were ceremonies or other circumstances.

I got married in my early 30s and my wife was 26. We have two sons. We have jobs. I am a tour guide and my wife works as hotel staff.

We have better income than our family farm, which gives us more opportunities to do what we could not do in the past.

Our children have better nutrition and education and also more facilities, which we did not have when we were their age. What we get allows us to do more things for other family, too.

We are family-oriented. Family is above all, so when they see that we have more, they will come to ask for help financially! Sometimes we give them but not all they want.

When we were in the village, if someone came from a city, we all gathered to listen to his or her stories. We were very amazed by the stories. And now with the technology, internet, and mobile phone, it is not possible to do that. We can communicate anytime, even to invite someone to come to attend our wedding is enough by phone.

In the past, we had to come to meet face to face to show respect and honor. Even to propose to a girl is able through the phone. And much more.

What has been the most important event in your country in your lifetime?

In my opinion, the big event in my country was the tsunami in Aceh in 2004. Two hundred thousand people lost their lives. It was very, very sad!

The other event that happened in Bali in 2002 was the terrorist bombing! A big bomb blew up in Kuta and took 200 peoples' lives. It was a horror for Bali!

How has your view of work changed over time?

The work has changed very fast since the IT grows. I was born in the 1960s and not very familiar with that. I face a shock and the problem is I am lazy to learn. I am so dependent on my wife and children, who are good in using a laptop or PC!

Tell me about your family:

I married my wife in 1995 and a year later we had the first son. We name him I Gusti Putu

Vidya Santosa and nearly four years later our second son was born. His name is I Gusti Made Vidnyana Subhakara. They graduated from a college in Bali and both of them studied tourism. The first son already works in hotel management and his brother just freshly graduated! I had a grandmother and grandfather who had a big vision as farmers that all their children and grandchildren have to get a better education, so that's why they sent me to the city to study. Family life has changed.

What is the most important lesson your family taught you?

The best lesson they taught me is we have to work together to accomplish the objective! My grandfather had land and he said to my uncle and my father that the land must not be divided as long as we still have children who study.

Work on the land and use the result to pay for the studies and family needs! By that way we could go to a higher school!

What's your biggest fear?

My biggest fear is when we are old and get sick and have no money!

What is your greatest pride?

My greatest pride is when I witnessed my wife give birth to both my children. And then when my older son is able to pass his bad habit (he was addicted to online gaming) and he is independent and mature now!

What was the favorite time of your life?

I have a good time when I am capable of doing what I like by myself. I like adventures. I climbed Mount Agung in Bali (3,142 meters above sea level) alone, ride my mountain bike around the island alone, etc.

What is the best decision you made?

Marrying my wife. I was close to three girls and I decided to marry her, not the other two. She is very simple and not demanding! She makes me very confident and is a convenience!

Do you have a hidden talent?

I like doing something what others do not want to do. I am a SCUBA instructor and was teaching at school once!

What advice do you have for the next generation?

My message to the young people is: Do what you like and be good to others, too! Do not be selfish.

Australia

Firoz K. "Phil" Pestonji

Place of Birth:
Valsad, Gujarat, India

Current Residence:
Perth, Western Australia, Australia

What is the best thing about where you live?

Peaceful, quiet yet a fully developed metropolis with all opportunities and the best of options.

How has life changed in your country since you were a child?

In India, things have changed so much for the better, especially in last 20 years: Modernization, public awareness, less corruption, improved cleanliness and general upliftment of people, etc.

In Perth and overall Australia, things are more progressive. Peoples' mentality and acceptance of multiculturalism has improved tremendously. There are more opportunities for younger people and the overall progression has improved.

What has been the most important event in your country in your lifetime?

The improvement in jobs in mining and oil and gas are taking front and center stage in Australia. Life is better overall.

How has your view of work changed over time?

With age I have become more sober, retracted and taking a more sedate view of life. Accept things better as they come.

Tell me about your family:

I have my wife and three grownup children, all in Perth or close by. They all are well-grounded and settled in their lives.

What is the most important lesson that your family taught you?

Work hard and work honestly, with patience and perseverance. At all times stand for truth, acceptance and dignity.

What's your biggest fear?

None and never had. Have utmost faith in God.

What is your greatest pride?

Assisting others when possible and gaining satisfaction from it.

What was the favorite time of your life?

Being a teenager in India and my engineering days in my 20s in Mumbai.

What is the best decision you made?

Too many to enumerate, but I keep going with the flow.

Do you have a hidden talent?

I am looking for it — hahahaha. I am an engineer, entrepreneur, researcher, author, community worker, etc.

What advice do you have for the next generation?

Work smart, work honestly, always assist others. Karma will reward you.

THE PINNACLES, NAMBUNG NATIONAL PARK, WESTERN AUSTRALIA, AUSTRALIA

TOBIAS KELLER/UNSPLASH

personal time is too important. I feel very fortunate to be in this position.

Tell me about your family:

I have not been particularly close to my own family since adulthood. I left the United Kingdom when I was 23, only returning for occasional holidays, weddings and funerals. I had a middle-class upbringing, a fairly happy childhood, with lots of family travel in the UK and quite a bit in Europe but not in a close extended-family environment.

My mother was English, from rural East Anglia, and she was a very gentle woman who passed away quite suddenly around 20 years ago. My Welsh father (recently deceased) was a rather brusque and bossy man. He supported me greatly and was very proud of me as I completed my education and traveled overseas with my career.

We spent some quality time together over the years (particularly after my mother passed away) but I could never quite shake the memories of his dominating presence, family arguments, and the feeling of anxiety in my childhood home.

I have a "new" family in Australia. My husband has kids from a previous marriage, now very much grown up, and they absolutely accept me into their family, which is wonderful.

What is the most important lesson that your family taught you?

To be grateful, polite and helpful to others. Acts of kindness are available to everyone.

What is the best thing about where you live?

The varied and natural environment, plus the relatively laid-back yet active lifestyle.

How has life changed in your country since you were a child?

Australia has become much more multicultural. It has shifted from a predominantly European origin population to a more diverse multicultural population with migrants from all around the world, in particular from our nearer neighbors in the Asia region (which I love). Although Australia still struggles with its somewhat tragic and uncomfortable history, there is now a much wider understanding of our First Nations history, their contributions and the challenges ahead.

What has been the most important event in your country in your lifetime?

That would be "The Apology" in 2008 — when then-Prime Minister Kevin Rudd made a formal apology to the indigenous "Stolen Generations" (the tragic policy from 1905 to 1967 that forcibly removed mixed-blood aboriginal children from their families).

How has your view of work changed over time?

I've always been a hard and conscientious worker, giving it my full attention, and often enjoying working away from home. But once I left my last full-time role (a few years ago), I soon realized that I never wanted to work full-time again. My

Australia
David George

Place of Birth:
Birmingham, England, United Kingdom

Current Residence:
Cairns, Queensland, Australia

What's your biggest fear?

My biggest personal fear would be to lose my eyesight. My biggest general fear is for the environmental challenges that our grandkids will face.

What is your greatest pride?

My photography, in particular my underwater photography, which is a great passion of mine.

What was the favorite time of your life?

When I spent a year or so managing a SCUBA diving center in Muscat, Sultanate of Oman, around 1997. I was single, independent, enjoying the hard-working life of a SCUBA instructor and a manager in a beautiful part of the world. I nearly stayed — but had a migration visa for Australia and a limited time to take it up.

What is the best decision you made?

My decision to migrate to Australia. It was not my intention to stay; I was quite nomadic really and came here for professional work. I fully expected to stay for three to five years and then head to another overseas location, but I am so glad that I decided to stay.

Do you have a hidden talent?

I can juggle fire clubs.

What advice do you have for the next generation?

Find out how things work, then you can fix them yourself.

Australia

Charles Akkary

Place of Birth:
Sydney, Australia

Current Residence:
Sydney is home but I am nomadic right now and plan to travel full-time for a few years before settling down on the central coast of New South Wales, Australia.

What is the best thing about where you live?

In Sydney you are never far from great food and open green space. Even though it's a huge city with a population of more than 5 million and all the diversity that that offers, in under an hour you can be in a gorgeous national park surrounded by nature.

You can also buy authentic-tasting food from pretty much any place on Earth!

How has life changed in your country since you were a child?

Australia has always been a land of homeowners. You grew up, traveled for a year or two, and then settled down and bought your own home. This was the Australian dream.

Today it's all but impossible for young people like our daughters to be able to do this without either significant help from their families or an extremely high-paying job and a steely determination to put everything they have into this goal (often at the expense of having kids or enjoying a balanced lifestyle).

What has been the most important event in your country in your lifetime?

It's hard to pinpoint a single event. The recognition of Aboriginal People as citizens and their right to vote in the late 1960s was the first step on a very slow path to equality, which still has miles to go.

The Mabo land rights decision (in the 1990s) and the government apology to the Stolen Generation in 2008 were positive steps but the recent unsuccessful vote to give indigenous people a voice in parliament was disappointing. Legalization of same-sex marriage in 2017 was another important human-rights milestone.

How has your view of work changed over time?

When I was younger I had to work in jobs I didn't really love to make ends meet. As I became more financially secure, I have been able to make choices about the type of work I do and how much of it.

I have recently decided to retire early (60 instead of the usual 67 in Australia). Not because I am wealthy but because I have enough to survive and I want to spend some time seeing the world (on a budget!).

Tell me about your family:

My parents emigrated from Lebanon independently before they married. They met in Australia and married in the early 1960s. I am the second oldest in a family of six, two boys and two girls. We have a very large and close-knit extended family that is very important to me.

I was a late bloomer and married my wife, Paula, when I was 38 years old. I have two adult stepdaughters and two wonderful grandchildren. Family is central to my life and I feel that not seeing them as much while I travel over the next few years will be the biggest challenge of this new lifestyle.

What is the most important lesson that your family taught you?

Respect for others regardless of their background or position in society. Everyone has a story to tell and a right to be heard.

What's your biggest fear?

Not keeping my health, not aging well. I make an effort to look after myself in regard to food and exercise and do all I can to maintain my health so I can enjoy the next 20 years of my life and not lose opportunities to continue exploring the world.

What is your greatest pride?

Making the national indoor soccer team and representing Australia for seven years.

What was the favorite time of your life?

The last 10 years have been my best. I was born in Australia but spent my adolescence in Brazil. I returned to Australia at 27 and did not travel again until I was 45 years old. Exploring and learning about new places and cultures makes me incredibly happy.

What is the best decision you made?

Leaving Brazil to return to Australia was by far the best decision I ever made. My life there was going nowhere, I didn't finish school or have a job and lived a chilled-out but uninspired life playing soccer on the beach.

Returning here and ultimately saving enough money to bring my family back and start my life again was key.

Do you have a hidden talent?

I can speak five languages quite fluently and I have a knack for picking up basic conversational skills within a few weeks of being in a new place.

What advice do you have for the next generation?

Prioritize your health. It's a cliche but nothing is more important than good health for a happy life. Strive for balance of work and play in your life.

Make an effort to maintain your friendships; people — not things — are what will make your life rich.

Embrace differences, and keep challenging yourself and stepping outside your comfort zone. This is what feeds your soul and keeps you young.

Australia
Terrence Harmse

Place of Birth:
Brakpan, Transvaal, South Africa

Current Residence:
Mackay, Queensland, Australia (since 2006)

What is the best thing about where you live?
Australia is a very socially diverse and tolerant country. My family and I have been made to feel very welcome here.

How has life changed in your country since you were a child?
We were last in South Africa in 2018 and noticed a lot of degradation of infrastructure and services.

What has been the most important event in your country in your lifetime?
Nothing of immense news seems to happen in Australia. I think this is what I really enjoy about it. It's predictable.

How has your view of work changed over time?
I have always believed that if I don't enjoy my work, I should do something else. I have re-invented myself continually over the years. Some of the things I have done: Started an apprenticeship (fitter and turner), a National Service SA Medical Services instructor, sold brakes and clutches and photocopiers, a firefighter/paramedic for 13 years, worked in engineering, self-employed as a fencer, a commercial diver, a heavy-truck driver, a health and safety advisor in the mining industry, a driving instructor, and a mine-dump truck operator. I still don't know what I would like to do.

Tell me about your family:
I am married to Penny and have twins born in 1999 and a stepdaughter and step-son and three step-grandsons whom I adore. My mother, an older brother and a younger brother and their families still live in South Africa.

What is the most important lesson that your family taught you?
To cherish each day because there's no guarantees.

What's your biggest fear?
I can't say that I have fears, but getting older has made me aware of my vulnerability and I hope that I will be around to see my kids have children.

What is your greatest pride?
That my children and step-children have turned out to be great people and contribute to society meaningfully.

What was the favorite time of your life?
I thoroughly enjoyed the 1980s as it was my formative years, doing national service and becoming a firefighter/paramedic. And we had the best music!

What is the best decision you made?
Deciding to emigrate to Australia.

Do you have a hidden talent?
I am definitely a jack-of-all-trades but certainly not a master. I believe I can do everything.

What advice do you have for the next generation?
As I told my kids, I don't care what they do in life as long as they contribute to society.

New Zealand

Paul McSharry

Place of Birth:
Christchurch, South Island, New Zealand

Current Residence:
Auckland, North Island, New Zealand

Tell me about your family:
My father was an Irish immigrant and my maternal grandparents were also Irish. In order

of age, my siblings are Patrick, Sean (deceased), Michael, Maureen, Paul, Bernadette, Therese, Philip (deceased), Kevin and Joseph. As children we had two choices for activities besides school and church: Irish dancing or boxing.

What is the best thing about where you live?
Auckland is the "City of Sails" with two harbors and 1.6 million residents. All the big stuff comes to Auckland.

What is the most important lesson that your family taught you?
Religion and how to use it.

What is your biggest fear?
More deaths in my family, including my own.

What is your greatest pride?
My 14-year-old daughter, Aaliyah.

What was your favorite time of your life?
My forties. In between marriages.

What is the best decision you made?
Got on the property market early.

Do you have hidden talent?
I started boxing in 1972 and I've not left yet.

What advice do you have for the next generation?
Cryptocurrency is good but don't put your eggs in one basket; you can't beat bricks and mortar. And your chromosomes determine what you are, not who you are.

How has life changed in your country since you were a child?
New Zealand doesn't resemble the country I was lucky to be born in. We're at the bottom of the world and we felt sheltered from the rest of the world's problems. We have the same problems today.

What has been the most important event in your country in your lifetime?
The Crown acknowledging the injustice to the confiscation of land and the colonization of the Māori people that has not been that beneficial to them. Fixing it is a burden for all New Zealand for generations to come.

How has your view of work changed over time?
I'm a spender. If I had considered a time when my income would someday lessen, maybe I might have put more of it away? Maybe not? I'm lucky — my wife's a saver.

New Zealand

Will Topia

Place of Birth:
Tāmaki Makaurau, Aotearoa (Auckland, New Zealand)

Current Residence:
Tāmaki Makaurau, Aotearoa (Auckland, New Zealand)

you were a child?

Population growth, technology, cost of living, environmental awareness, obsessive personal presentation.

What has been the most important event in your country in your lifetime?

The impact of Covid-19; the loss of loved ones, economic struggles, and the long journey it's taking to rebuild.

How has your view of work changed over time?

Not being in a position for an early retirement, there is more focus to remain in the workforce. I am fortunate to co-own a small business, which offers a sense of job security, but the work still needs to be done.

We are now at an age where employment life expectancy in a corporate role is relatively short, no matter what one's experience, skill factor, dedication, and loyalty is. Baby Boomers are slowly (with reluctance) being pushed aside for the Gen X, Millennials, and Gen Z generations.

Tell me about your family:

We are proud Maori descendants of the Ngapuhi tribe from Panguru, Hokianga (Far North). I am the youngest of 12: six boys and six girls. Within the past four years we have lost four siblings: two boys and two girls. Our parents were

What is the best thing about where you live?

There's nothing like home. The Kiwi way of life.

How has life changed in your country since

staunch Catholics; everything revolved around the church.

Our humble upbringing in Auckland gave us a roof over our heads and food on the table. Whilst dad was the "bread maker," mum looked after the younger children and ruled the house.

She insisted the eldest girls took care of everything inside the house, and the boys were tasked with everything outside, including maintaining the grounds of the church and local convent.

Our family homestead gatherings, generally following church services, were sensational. So much fun, food, and enjoyment. Our neighbors would join us, and the backyard would become the local playground for cricket, basketball, rugby and so much more. The three eldest grandchildren (two boys, one girl) grew up in the same household, the age gap between the four of us is just six years. I've always regarded these three as my younger siblings.

When we lost our dad in 1978, he left a gaping hole which was emotionally and mentally tough on the family, none more so than our mum. To her credit, she lived for many more years (to 2003), to see the paths her *tamariki* (children) and *mokopuna* (grandchildren) would take, whilst retaining her faith to her final day.

We are blessed with what they both instilled in all of us, which has filtered through to grandchildren and great-grandchildren. People often say it must be wonderful coming from a big family. For the warm, loving memories definitely, but when a loss occurs, it hits hard. And then you think, there are more to come. That's not so wonderful. God bless. Rest in love, mum, dad, brothers, and sisters.

What is the most important lesson that your family taught you?
Treat everyone equal.

What's your biggest fear?
Aging and being reliant on support and care from others.

What is your greatest pride?
My mum and dad, for the legacy they built in our church and neighborhood and for teaching me right from wrong.

What was the favorite time of your life?
Every day above ground is a favorite time of life.

What is the best decision you made?
Business co-ownership.

Do you have a hidden talent?
Caring for others less fortunate.

What advice do you have for the next generation?
Live a happy and positive life because one day you, too, might have an opportunity to participate in an *Around the World in Sixty Years* questionnaire!

New Zealand

Jonathan Mower

Place of Birth:
Essex, England

Current Residence:
Auckland, New Zealand

What is the best thing about where you live?

Location. Auckland is situated on an isthmus between two great harbors, one of which opens into the Hauraki Gulf with its many islands, some of which are conservation sanctuaries that are home to populations of some of our endangered *taonga* (treasure) species.

Also near to Auckland are the Waitakere Ranges, a sprawling national park forest growing over an ancient volcanic mountain range with many tracks that allow easy access to native forest and isolated beaches. Ironically, the best thing about living in Auckland is that it is easy to escape it and find peaceful, quiet sanctuaries elsewhere. Although I live in a city, I usually find that the best places are where other people aren't.

How has life changed in your country since you were a child?

It has become more culturally diverse. I grew up in a small town in the Bay of Plenty with a largely bi-cultural population that was perhaps 60 percent European and 40 percent Māori. Now I live in a city that has a far more diverse cultural blend.

At the same time, it has become much less egalitarian, with a much greater divide between the haves and the have-nots, which is a great shame as socially the country has lost a great deal in the process.

Through a combination of the growth of large-scale, fertilizer-intensive agriculture (in particular the dairy industry), an increasing population and aging infrastructure, the waterways of this country have in many cases suffered a great loss of integrity and are suffering health-wise.

When we were kids, we could stop the car, get out and go for in a swim in most of the waterways we came across, but sadly that is no longer the case.

What has been the most important event in your country in your lifetime?

It is difficult to answer this as there have been many things that have happened in my lifetime that have had significant effects. I think this country's decision to begin to rectify a long list of wrongs that were done to the Māori, the first people of this land, would be one of the most important.

Signed in 1840, the Treaty of Waitangi was written and signed by the Crown and the leaders of Māori *iwi* (tribes) but it was massively compromised after signing, profoundly diminishing and disenfranchising Māori as people in their own country.

For years now, the Crown has been working to accept and apologize for the wrongs that were subsequently done, offering different forms of compensation. This has had a profound effect on much of this country, with Māori culture and *reo* (language) now being much more visible than it used to be.

In many ways, New Zealand has become more accepting of its place in the world as a country of the South Pacific, rather than as an outpost of Great Britain.

How has your view of work changed over time?

I have been in customer-service-based work for most of my life and a while ago realized that this wasn't going to give me a high-paying career. I have seen people around me pass away very young, many of whom had great jobs, high-stress jobs that came with a lot of *mana* (prestige), and I have come to understand that home life and good health are worth more than a big income.

Life is short enough as it is and who needs a port hole in their coffin?

Tell me about your family:

We emigrated to this country when I was 4 — Mum, Dad and four boys.

Growing up in a small town meant we were lucky to be gifted a great childhood, with hard-working parents and a very outdoorsy lifestyle.

We had great and supportive parents, which molds the way you look at the world.

We are all now much older and still have both our parents in our lives. My brothers have been very successful in their lives and careers and now have grandchildren.

As kids we were lucky. Very lucky, actually.

What is the most important lesson that your family taught you?

There are many to choose from but that you should treat people with respect is definitely one of them. Have good manners because good manners will open doors in life; be truthful to yourself and don't say things that you wouldn't want to have repeated.

What is your greatest pride?

Being with my partner for 28 years.

What was the favorite time of your life?

The last 10 years would be up there. Relatively late in life, I discovered birding and ran with that ball as it seemed to suit my view of life nicely.

About 10 years ago, I began volunteering one day a week on Tiritiri Matangi, a conservation sanctuary island near Auckland that is home to some of New Zealand's rarest bird and reptile species. It is an open sanctuary and a place of scientific research.

It runs many public education programs and I get to take people, including school kids, for guided walks, help with island maintenance and take part in a number of the island's conservation programs.

Being able to volunteer there meant I had a near vertical learning curve, and in return it allowed me to share insights and teach people how rare and special much of this country's flora and fauna are.

I have also been able take part in some of the island's conservation programs and have met many interesting people from a surprising array of countries.

Later in life, I learned that picking up a camera allowed you to show people things that you find beautiful and interesting, and that has added an extra aspect to my volunteering on the island.

What is the best decision you made?

That is a broad question. Being a poster child for Librans, it takes me a long time to weigh things up before making decisions, but finally coming to grips with things and coming out to live as a gay man would be up there.

I was lucky to have such a supportive family and to live in the country that I do, as they made the decision easier than it is for many other people in the world.

Do you have a hidden talent?

Not that I have found as yet, but there is always room for self-discovery. After all, you don't stop learning until you stop breathing.

What advice do you have for the next generation?

Be honest and respectful to yourself, to those that love you, and to the world around you.

Life is short and we only have one world, so try to leave it in a better state than when you arrived.

Samoa
Kevin Patrick Hartin

Place of Birth:
Melbourne, Australia

Current Residence:
Asaga Village, Savai'i, Samoa

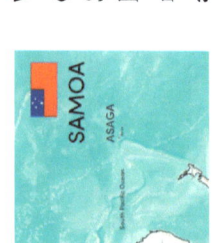

What is the best thing about where you live?

Samoa offers a simple lifestyle, great weather for my old bones and I live amongst some of the happiest and content people I have ever experienced in my 61 years.

So many aspects of current life in Samoa remind me of life in Australia in my teenage and early adult years, when life was far less complicated and more easygoing. In the 10 years I have lived in Samoa, I have never worn shoes, socks or long pants and more often than not I get around in a pair of shorts, optional shirt and a pair of thongs.

How has life changed in your country since you were a child?

Australia is almost unrecognizable from when I was a child. Back in the 1970s Australia was a bit of a civilized backwater compared to western nations like the United States or the United Kingdom. With the passing of time, adoption of technology and advances in transport, Australia is now no different to the U.S. or U.K. Having been out of Australia for 10 years, I hardly recognize it from when I left.

Samoa, on the other hand, is still 20 to 30 years behind Australia in many ways, apart from mobile phones, where we are only five years behind. A major difference is that Samoa is still very much a cash-based society, where you can still write checks for your purchases.

What has been the most important event in your country in your lifetime?

In my 10 years in Samoa, we had a change in government after more than 25 years back in 2020, which has allowed many of the things that previously held Samoa's development back to slowly move forward.

Also, Samoa locked down pretty hard in April 2020 for Covid, only opening borders in September 2022, which made it very tough for us in the tourism sector but proud that it was not until March 2022 that we had our first case of community transmission.

How has your view of work changed over time?

I spent 30 years in what was the most progressive and fast-moving sector of information technology. I worked my way up the ladder and ended up working excessive hours for many years, which in hindsight was OK but not sustainable. Now I have my own business in the tourism sector, renting scooters to tourists, which allows me much more flexibility and I am now finally working to live rather than living to work.

Tell me about your family:

My parents were "10-pound tourists" coming from Ireland via England to Australia in the late 1950s when Australia was screaming out for immigrants. After working hard for about five or six years, Dad ended up buying an excavator and started working for himself on contract to the many Irishmen building roads, gas lines and water mains in a fast-growing Melbourne.

Mum gave up work when I came along in 1963 and my brother followed in 1966, looking after our little family and supporting Dad's efforts by doing the books. Life was great in Melbourne and we ended up with a holiday place in the country, where motorbikes and water skiing were the usual weekend activities.

Cancer took Mum in 2000 and Dad remarried about seven years later, having moved to the beach side suburbs of Melbourne where he is still going at the age of 91. I have a son from my first marriage who is in his early 30s now, as does my current wife, plus we have a 15-year-old son here in Samoa.

What is the most important lesson that your family taught you?

Hard work and honesty will eventually win our doing things I had given up 10 years earlier and between marriages.

What's your biggest fear?

My father passing away while I'm here in Samoa. Back in the 1970s my Mum made a dash back to Ireland as her dad was dying, only to get there about two hours late due to some delays in England. At least we have video calls.

What is your greatest pride?

My sons.

What was the favorite time of your life?

My mid-30s — good job, cash in my pocket, doing things I had given up 10 years earlier and between marriages.

What is the best decision you made?

Moving to Samoa 10 years ago.

Do you have a hidden talent?

If I do, it has been hiding for the last 61 years!

What advice do you have for the next generation?

Carpe diem — seize the day — as you never know what tomorrow will bring. Also, do not let others dictate your happiness; follow your head as well as your heart, work hard, and be good to others and you will find happiness.

BEACH HUTS, SAVAI'I, SAMOA
©CORNERS74/DREAMSTIME

MORNING RAINBOW OVER APIA, SAMOA
©RAMUNAS BRUZAS/DREAMSTIME

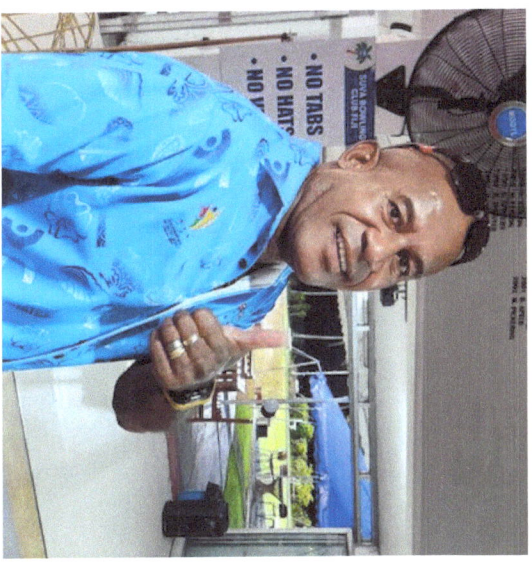

Fiji

Waisea Turaga

Place of Birth:
Suva, Fiji

Current Residence:
Fiji

What is the best thing about where you live?
God.

What's your biggest fear?
God.

What is your greatest pride?
My children.

What was the favorite time of your life?
When I represented Fiji in the World Bowls Champion vs Champion lawn bowling tournament in Australia seven years ago.

Do you have a hidden talent?
I can drink with anyone under the table!

What is the best decision you made?
When I changed my life, from hanging out on the streets to becoming a professional sportsman.

How has life changed in your country since you were a child?
I still haven't changed, lol.

What has been the most important event in your country in your lifetime?
Fiji won three consecutive titles in the Hong Kong Sevens rugby tournament in 1990, 1991 and 1992.

How has your view of work changed over time?
I gained so many new friendships.

Tell me about your family:
I am married with four kids and six grandchildren.

What advice do you have for the next generation?
Be patient, be kind, and love each other.

What is the most important lesson that your family taught you?
To be patient and to be kind.

About the Author

John S. Wolfe

Place of Birth:
Rochester, New York, United States

Current Residence:
Tempe, Arizona, United States

What is the best thing about where you live?
300 days of sunshine (which gives people a reason to smile)! And great golf!

How has life changed in your country since you were a child?
The 1970s were pre-cable television, pre-internet, pre-cellphones, and pre- ever-present media. You lived in your small world and didn't know about — or care about — much else. Now we know everyone else's business but struggle to find meaning in ours.

What has been the most important event in your country in your lifetime?
I cite three:

- Landing on the moon in 1969. It was an incredible technological achievement with what looks like now were primitive tools. It gave the entire nation inspiration that anything was possible — and men and women would push the envelope in virtually every field in the subsequent decades.

- 9/11. I select this because the act of terrorism contributed to a sense of vulnerability that Americans were feeling at the new millennium, with the new internet disrupting traditional industries like real estate, retailing, banking, advertising and media. The uncertainty led to a need for immediate gratification among younger generations, a condition that was then exacerbated by the introduction of social media and a focus on one's self-image.

- The Covid-19 pandemic. To see a country — let alone the entire world — turn itself off was something I didn't expect to experience and hope to never again. In the U.S., in my opinion, all levels of government assumed too much authority to "protect the citizenry" — and it will be a challenge for them to give back that power.

How has your view of work changed over time?
My first job was teaching canoeing at a summer camp. That was fun.

For 20 years after college I put together weekly newspapers for small communities. That was fun.

After going back to school for an MBA, my wife and I ran a unique gift shop serving visitors to Arizona. That was fun. Work is easier to do when you enjoy it.

Tell me about your family:
My wife, Michelle, and I met in college and have been married for 38 years. She has been the catalyst for many of our adventures, going back to our honeymoon in Switzerland and a visit to Hong Kong in 1994.

We have two daughters, who are successful and in committed relationships. When the six of us get together, there are a lot of laughs.

We also have six "exchange daughters," girls from France, Germany, Thailand, Turkey, Egypt, and Turkmenistan who each spent a school year with us and with whom we stay in touch. The first one, from France, delivered a baby girl in 2023.

My parents had me when they were about 40. My father was a local journalist and my mother was a community volunteer. They divorced about 10 years after I was born and I lived with my mother. After college I worked for my father, who died in 1999. My mother died in 2008. I think of her often.

What is the most important lesson that your family taught you?

The Sibley family on my mother's side came from England in 1629. My great-grandfather started a dry-goods store in Rochester, New York in 1868 that grew into a department store, Sibley's. Along the way the family created a crest with Cicero's phrase, *esse quam videri* — "to be rather than to seem." I took it to mean, be true to yourself in whatever you do.

What's your biggest fear?

A debilitating health problem that burdens my wife and children.

What is your greatest pride?

My girls. Family took priority over work when they were younger and it was time well spent, based on who they are today.

What was the favorite time of your life?

Without much planning, my life can be broken down into decades, based on what I was doing. This current period is my favorite, as we were able to retire and set out on a bucket-list item — an around-the-world cruise — in 2023. And that led to this book.

What is the best decision you made?

Marrying my wife. She has the focus and discipline I wish I had.

Do you have a hidden talent?

It's not singing.

What advice do you have for the next generation?

I told my daughters when they went to college: Do whatever you want to do. Pursue relationships that nourish you, interests that fulfill you, and careers that support the life you desire. Be generous with your love.

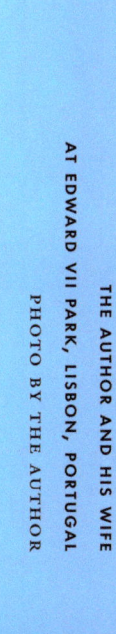

THE AUTHOR AND HIS WIFE
AT EDWARD VII PARK, LISBON, PORTUGAL
PHOTO BY THE AUTHOR

NOW IT'S YOUR TURN

What is the best thing about where you live?

How has life changed in your country since you were a child?

What has been the most important event in your country in your lifetime?

How has your view of work changed over time?

Name:

Place of Birth:

Current Residence:

Tell me about your family:

_____

_____

What is the most important lesson that your family taught you?

_____

_____

_____

What's your biggest fear?

_____

_____

_____

What is your greatest pride?

_____

_____

_____

What was the favorite time of your life?

_____

_____

What is the best decision you made?

_____

_____

Do you have a hidden talent?

_____

_____

What advice do you have for the next generation?

_____

_____

_____

ATACAMA DESERT, ANTOFAGASTA, CHILE
DIEGO JIMENEZ/UNSPLASH

MAY THE ROAD rise to meet you,
May the wind be always at your back.
May the sun shine warm upon your face,
The rains fall soft upon your fields.
And, until we meet again,
May God hold you in the palm
Of His hand.

AUTHOR UNKNOWN